...It's Where You Played the Game

How Youth Baseball Determines the Personality of the American Male

**Mike Ryan
and
Luke Ryan**

HENRY HOLT AND COMPANY   NEW YORK

Henry Holt and Company, Inc.
Publishers since 1866
115 West 18th Street
New York, New York 10011

Henry Holt® is a registered
trademark of Henry Holt and Company, Inc.

Published in Canada by Fitzhenry & Whiteside Ltd.,
195 Allstate Parkway, Markham, Ontario L3R 4T8.

Library of Congress Cataloging-in-Publication Data
Ryan, Mike.
. . . it's where you played the game: how youth baseball
determines the personality of the American male/
Mike Ryan and Luke Ryan.—1st ed.
1. Baseball for children—United States—Psychological
aspects. 2. Men—United States—Psychology. 3. Personality.
I. Ryan, Luke. II. Title.
GV880.4.R93   1996   95-47641
796.323'07'7—dc20   CIP

ISBN 0-8050-4661-5

Henry Holt books are available for special promotions and
premiums. For details contact: Director, Special Markets.

First Edition—1996

Designed by Paula R. Szafranski

Printed in the United States of America
All first editions are printed on acid-free paper.∞

10 9 8 7 6 5 4 3 2 1

To
Jerry Fitzsimons, shortstop, 1946–1971
Pete Theberge, shortstop, 1972–1988

Contents

Contents

1

The Roots of Baseballism

It is in games that many men discover their Paradise. —*Robert Lynd*

And their Hades . . .   —*The authors*

My name is Mike. I am forty-nine years old. I am a baseballholic. My twenty-three-year-old son is named Luke. He, too, is a baseballholic. We suffer from a disease called baseballism. There is no known treatment and no possible cure. The condition is chronic but mercifully not fatal, though some days we, the afflicted and infected, wish it were. There is no need for panic in the general populace, as the disease is not contagious. You either have it or you don't. Medical science cannot agree whether the cause is environmental or genetic, but the prevalent theory is that some are born with a genetic predisposition or vulnerability to baseballism and environmental factors then determine who ultimately contracts the affliction.

While we acknowledge that baseballism is a disease of denial, neither Luke nor I knew we were ill until the summer of 1994 when the major leaguers went out on strike. Until then, baseball was so abundant and available in the schools, workplaces, and streets of America, we blended in with the casual users and never noticed our dependency. Same thing happened to boozers in 1919. Prior to Prohibition, thousands of Americans were ignorant of their dependence on alcohol. Soon as it was outlawed, they began swilling bathtub gin, hair tonics, and cough medicines.

When the major leaguers took to the picket lines, in a manner of speaking, the consequential withdrawal turned Luke and me into raving maniacs. Without morning box scores, we broke into cold sweats and tremors. Our body temperatures dropped and we became irritable, sometimes irrational, for the entire day.

Without game highlights on the eleven o'clock news, we both became insomniacs. Our relationships suffered, our work productivity dropped, our food intake decreased. At the time, he was living in New York City and I in western Massachusetts, so neither was aware of the other's distress and neither recognized that the source of the malady was the strike. Luke will explain how we saw the light. I will reveal how we sank into darkness.

Baseball had always been our common bond, the cement of our relationship. We were Red Sox fans, charter members of the Fenway Faithful, and made every home opener from '79 to '91, our streak finally broken when Luke moved away to go to college. Even through his teenage years, when we fought over his messy bedroom, curfews, grades, allowance, his comrades of choice, and his batting stance, we could take in a ball game and revel in each other's companionship, comfortable, content, and connected by our common passion.

Each of us marked the passing of our days by baseball events. I was born in '46, the year Ted Williams came back from the war and led the Sox to the pennant; the year Enos Slaughter scored from first base while Pesky held the ball and the Red Sox lost the

Series in seven. I was only two months old when it happened but I swear I remember it.

In 1954, I began playing baseball for Local 263. I was the starting second baseman and I began every day by opening the newspaper to check the stats of my hero, Red Sox second baseman Ted Lepcio. It gave me great comfort that my own stats were almost as good as his. The year I graduated from high school, Bill Monbouquette threw five shutouts and I saw two of them. That was the same year Ebbetts Field fell to the wrecking ball. The army drafted me in '67 when Jim Lonborg, pitching on two days' rest, ran out of gas and the Cardiac Kids lost the Series to the Cards. I was married the day the Red Sox bought Ron Kline from the Giants, and though both relationships started with high hopes and great expectations, mine proved to be longer, happier, and more productive.

Luke was born in '72, shortly after the first baseball strike delayed the start of season and ultimately cost the Red Sox the pennant when they finished a half game behind Detroit; the year Pudge Fisk broke into the majors as Rookie of the Year. Luke was three in '75 when Fisk's twelfth-inning home run tied the World Series at three games apiece. Twenty-four hours later when Joe Morgan's bloop single brought the title to the Big Red Machine, I cried myself to sleep, swearing I would give up baseball forever to spare my son the agony of being a Red Sox fan. If only I had kept that pledge!

I tried. God knows I tried. For three years, I never watched a live televised baseball game if Luke was home. Often on Sunday afternoons, my wife Judy would take Luke to visit her parents so I could catch a game in the comfort of my couch, but other than that I went cold turkey. Well, okay, not completely. A few times when I claimed to be in Boston on business, I was sitting in the bleachers at Fenway Park, but I never checked box scores or watched game highlights in front of Luke. I shielded and protected him from baseball, particularly from the Red Sox. I even hid my Red Sox cap, souvenir programs, and pennants by putting them over the furnace in the cellar. Covered with Saran Wrap, of course.

One morning in the late spring of '78, Luke marched into the kitchen and announced that baseball tryouts were Saturday morning and he was thinking of playing. My heart sank into my shoes. Where had I failed? Hadn't I taken him fishing? Hadn't I kicked around the soccer ball with him until my leg felt like it would fall off? Hadn't I put up a Nerf basketball hoop in the living room? What more could a father do?

Judy was unconcerned. "What's the big deal?" she asked that night after we had safely tucked him into bed with visions of home runs dancing in his head.

"I don't want him to get hurt," I muttered.

"Hurt? The way you two play soccer it's a wonder he hasn't broken a leg."

"You don't understand," I tried to explain. "It's not his bones I worry about breaking. It's his heart."

The next night at supper, Luke was glowing like the Citgo sign behind Fenway's left field scoreboard.

"Did Mom tell you what we saw today?" he asked. Contrary to my repeated warnings, Judy had walked Luke down the south side of Main Street and he was drawn like a magnet to the window display of baseball gloves in Western Village Sports.

"She mentioned something," I admitted, glaring at his mother.

"Well, Dad? Huh? Huh? Can I get it? For my birthday? Is it okay?"

"Whoa," I cautioned. "Get what?"

"A Carl Yastrzemski glove! Dad, Yaz signed it himself!"

"What about that spinning rod you saw last week?"

"You can buy that for you, Dad, so you can fish while I'm playing baseball."

"C'mon," I said, "you love fishing. You don't even know anything about baseball."

"I know more than you!" Luke pouted, looking sideways at his mother. Judy stood up quickly and started to clear the dishes from the table, but I had seen the look of guilt in her eyes.

"Okay," I said rising to the challenge, "who was the last major leaguer to hit .400?"

"That's so easy," Luke said. "Ted Williams, 1941, .406. He also had a slugging percentage of .735, 185 hits, 37 home runs, 145 walks, and 120 RBIs. He should have won the American League MVP but the press didn't like him so it went to Joe DiMaggio, a damn Yankee."

Before I could recover from the shock, he shot one at me.

"What was the lowest batting average to ever win the American League batting title?"

"Yaz, '68, .301," I automatically snapped back. "How do you know this stuff?"

"Baseball cards," Luke answered. "I have the whole Topps collection."

So there we were. He was only six and we were standing at a crossroad. His path of choice was baseball. I could go along with him—sharing his hopes, his joys, his triumphs, and his inescapable misery—or I could go fishing by myself.

After he was asleep, Judy admitted that on Sunday afternoons while I was home watching the game on the tube, Luke was at her father's house watching the Sox with his grandfather. That's where he kept his baseball cards, too. I felt like a cuckold.

"If you can't lick 'em, join 'em," I reasoned. My own father, who was ten years old in 1918 when the Red Sox sold Babe Ruth to the Yankees, never sanctioned my interest in baseball and repeatedly warned me to control my enthusiasm for the game. Every time the Red Sox came up short—and the Red Sox came up short every time—he would shake his head and recite "Casey at the Bat," as if it were a biblical parable. He was wise, but his wisdom was a wedge, and I thought it better to share my son's suffering than impress him with my judgment.

So Luke brought his cards home. Sundays his maternal grandfather came over and the three of us watched games together. His paternal grandfather, the wise one, started calling our house "Mudville." For Luke's birthday, we gave him the Yastrzemski glove. He still has it, oiled and rolled in Saran Wrap, in his bottom drawer.

Luke tried out for the town youth league, but I stayed home, pacing and nervous, instinctively knowing the die of his life was being cast and that the numbers that came up would be permanently branded into his psyche. I couldn't watch. He left my house that day as a little boy. He came home a second baseman.

My first reaction was relief that he wasn't a right fielder, a pitcher, or a third baseman, followed by a blush of pride that he was following in my footsteps at the keystone sack. That's where my love of baseball, took seed in '54. Then in rapid succession came uneasiness, alarm, and panic. How could I save Luke from such pain if he, too, was destined to be a second baseman?

That's when I first realized the futility of trying to protect a child from life's dangers. No matter how careful a parent guides and shields his offspring, perils will be encountered. Warnings don't help; prohibitions don't work. Rant and rave, prance and preach, but once a kid tastes sugar, no amount of parental power, persuasion, or prayer can prevent him from gobbling candy and chugging colas every chance he gets. And candy is easy compared to sex, drugs, rock and roll, fried food, easy money, and baseball. Added to the frustration of parenting is the guilt of knowing that whether the cause is environmental or genetic, most apples fall right under the tree. Luke was my son and he was destined to be blue-eyed, bald, and tormented by baseball. Unless, of course, the team he loved became a perennial power like the 1950s Yankee teams.

The summer of '78 was blessed with fine weather, youth base-ball games, and a Boston baseball juggernaut. Luke batted number two and led his team in on-base percentage and base hits. In the field, he imagined himself Jerry Remy; at the plate, Jim Rice. When the mid-July American East pennant race showed the Red Sox with a commanding fourteen-game lead, Luke's enthusiasm ran rampant and rabid. I couldn't stop it; I went with the flow, even when the flow became a torrent. In August I took him to Fenway Park. We sat in right field, just behind the bullpen, and Luke brought his Carl Yastrzemski glove, expecting to catch a Yaz home run. Dennis Eckersley pitched a shutout, Rice homered over the Green Monster, and the Red Sox won, 6–0. Luke came home with his glove empty but his heart full.

A father's love is an intoxicant; it produces hallucinations so vivid the father forgets all life's lessons and believes his strangest fantasies. Our first day in Fenway was so sun-filled and success-ful, I believed the baseball gods had smiled on Luke and would never be so cruel as to disappoint him.

When the Red Sox held their lead over the fast-charging Yan-kees through August, I credited Luke's devotion. He was bringing the old home team good luck, and that was all they needed to erase the curse of selling the Babe. I wanted to be there with Luke when the old ghosts were finally and forever exorcised from Fenway Park. I bought two tickets from a local scalper for the fourth game of the September home series with the Yankees.

When September tenth arrived, the Red Sox were spiraling from their lofty lead over the Yankees like a MiG full of lead. In the previous three games, all Yankee victories, the Scarlet Hose had been outscored 35–5 by the Bronx Bombers and their lead was down to a single game. In retrospect, I was a damn fool, but at the time I sincerely believed that Luke's presence in Fenway would bring the Sox good luck and inspire them to victory. I have no other excuse for subjecting my beloved son to the carnage he witnessed. It was like bringing a child to a Spanish arena to cheer

7

for the bull against the matador. I had trouble finding a parking spot and we missed the first inning. As we trudged through the tunnels under the stands we could hear moans from the crowd, and when we emerged into the light, the Red Sox were behind 6–0. The Bataan March was a mild stroll through the woods compared to our hundred-mile drive home on the Mass Turnpike after the Red Sox were humiliated by the Yankees, 7–4. In the four-game must-win series, they had been outscored 42–9, committed more errors (11) than runs, and surrendered their four-game lead.

Romantic love is blind; paternal love is just plain stupid. When the Sox pulled themselves out of their spiral by winning thirteen of their last fifteen games to end the regular season in a dead-heat tie with the Yankees, I believed again. Worse, I let my son believe, too. A one-game playoff was scheduled for October second. I skipped work and Luke played hooky. I told him that bearing witness to a miraculous rebirth was more important than attending school. Together we huddled with both his grandfathers in our living room to watch the game. On the mound, it was Guidry in grays against Torrez in the whites. In my living room, it was history against hope.

When the Red Sox broke into an early lead, hope hopped over history and we started talking pitching matchups against the Royals in the ALCS. We were barely paying attention in the top of the seventh when an anemic-hitting shortstop in grays came to the plate with two on and two out. Bucky Dent had about as much chance of homering off Mike Torrez as our Olympic hockey team would have against Sweden or Russia.

Ouch! Dent's Fenway fly made it just over the wall, but it was 3–2 and, for all practical purposes, it was over. Still, hope springs eternal. When Yaz came to the plate with the tying run on third with two outs in the ninth, we knew the stage was set for the most dramatic home run in baseball history. It was perfect casting. Yaz had spent his youth dreaming of playing for the Yankees but they had insulted and spurned him. The Red Sox fall from grace in 1918 was caused by the Sox rejection of Ruth; their resurrection would come sixty years later off the bat of a Yankee reject. Balance. Irony. Salvation. Comeuppance. All Yaz had to do was hit the damn ball out of the park.

My father, with the sensitivity of a Star Chamber judge, began reciting "Casey at the Bat." It was an omen. Yaz popped out. Luke cried. I cursed. My father ad-libbed:

> *Oh, somewhere in this fabled land,*
> *The sun is shinning bright,*
> *The band is playing somewhere,*
> *And somewhere hearts are light;*
> *And somewhere men are laughing,*
> *And somewhere children shout,*
> *But there is no joy in Beantown:*
> *Yastrzemski has popped out.*

When Judy came home, Luke was sobbing in his bedroom. I was sitting at the kitchen table, surrounded by empty beer cans. Barely able to speak, I pointed upstairs, shrugged my shoulders, and began to cry.

"I tried to warn you," I moaned.

"Go fish," she said and ran upstairs to comfort her son.

2

The Effects of Baseballism

I'd go through hell in a gasoline suit to play baseball.   —*Pete Rose*

Cub fans are ninety percent scar tissue.   —*George Will*

My name is Luke. I am a baseballholic. I believe I was born with the disease of baseballism; it was in my paternal genes. I don't blame my father; he didn't know and could not have prevented it if he did. I'm just grateful I didn't inherit his hairline. It took me a long time to recognize my affliction and if it weren't for the baseball strike of '94, I'd probably still be blissfully ignorant of my dependence on the game. Let me tell you how I discovered my baseballism.

August 12, 1994, is a day that will live in infamy. It was the sixtieth anniversary of Babe Ruth's last game in Fenway Park, the twentieth anniversary of Nolan Ryan's nineteen-strikeout game against the Red Sox, and the first day of the strike that would cancel the 1994 World Series. Who knew?

I expected the walkout would last a week or two, possibly a month. I never conceived it possible there would not be a World Series. Why else have October? Why not just cancel autumn and skip everything from Labor Day to Thanksgiving?

I didn't understand my own reaction to the strike until the end of August. As a spring college grad without a job, I was busy planning my life, sending out résumés, learning to knot a tie, polishing my shoes, practicing my handshake and smile. I scored a couple of job interviews but bombed. I had always been comfortable with strangers, able to put others at ease with casual conversation and adept at social occasions, but in my interviews I became tongue-tied, hesitant, unsure of myself. Something was amiss but I couldn't get a handle on it.

Lying in bed one night staring at the ceiling, I started to cry. Grief swept over me and I sobbed like a baby, but my tears brought insight. Only twice before had I ever felt so bad—in '78 when Yaz popped out and in '86 when Buckner's error cost the Sox the Series. Suddenly I heard my grandfather's words echoing in my mind, "There is no joy in Beantown . . ." and I knew what was wrong in my life: there was no baseball.

I looked at the time. It was three thirty in the morning. "The hell with it," I said and called home.

"Sorry to wake you," I told my dad when he answered.

"You didn't," he interrupted. "I haven't been sleeping well and was just walking around the kitchen."

"How's your appetite?" I asked.

"Don't have one."

"Mom?"

"She's fine. I guess. We haven't been talking much lately."

"Work?"

"It sucks. I'm fighting with everyone."

"You know what's wrong?"

"Not a clue. I had a checkup, though; it's not physical. I'm just bummed out."

"Dad, I know how you feel. I've been going through the same thing. It's the damn baseball strike."

"Naw, c'mon."

"I'm serious. It got me, too. You know why I'm screwing up my interviews? No baseball. All my life I've started conversations by commenting on games or players or standings or trades, whatever I saw in the news. It's my entry, my passport. I can talk baseball with anyone but with no baseball, I got no ammunition. You, too."

He saw the light. We commiserated as only two old second basemen can. He quoted something Bill Lee said that made no sense. I don't remember the exact words but nothing Lee ever said made sense. I told him a funny Luis Tiant story. I don't remember which story but all Luis Tiant stories are funny. We talked for two hours, and for the first time since August 12 I felt better. I knew my problem. I understood my dilemma.

Everything I ever needed to know, I learned from baseball. I had a baseball adage to explain everything from atheism ("There are no atheists in the bleachers in the bottom of the ninth") to zoology ("Man is the only species in the animal kingdom that can love, hope, or hit a curveball").

Baseball became my frame of reference through which I viewed the world. My parents caught on to this quirk early and exploited it for their own purposes. While other kids were learning about the virtue in all people from the parable of the Good Samaritan, my mother taught the same principle with the story of the Good Yankee Fan.

My father told me baseball bedtime stories. Some of my favorites were "How Williams Won the MVP in 1941," "How Pesky Nailed Slaughter at Home," "How Lepcio Was Elected to the Hall of Fame," and "How Lonborg Won the Seventh on Two Days' Rest." By innocently repeating his revisionist histories, I caused myself great embarrassment and subjected myself to humiliating ridicule. Yet he would never even give me the satisfaction of an apology. "I didn't want you to have nightmares," he'd explain, as if that made everything okay.

My father stimulated in me a deeper understanding of human nature, from associations of particular mannerisms and attributes of my friends with the positions they played on my baseball team. Between the two of us, we developed a baseball-based philosophy that encompassed half of humanity—the male half. From what I could see, neither one of us had an explanation for the behaviors of women, which was mostly okay. He, being married to my mom, didn't need one, and I, a late bloomer, didn't understand the utility of such knowledge until it was too late.

Our philosophy provided insights into the male personality and gave us an edge in all our social interactions. It allowed us to predict behaviors in our peers, resulting in personal success in all contests from my hide-and-seek games to his political campaigns. We dubbed it our "ace in the hole."

By the time I reached adulthood, baseball formed the basis of my beliefs, ethics, and nature, but with the players on strike I was bereft of a self-identity. Without baseball, my abilities to comprehend, perceive, evaluate, articulate, enunciate, demonstrate, and interrelate were short-circuited. I was a boor. Worse, as a recent college graduate, I was unemployable.

A few days after discovering the cause of my malaise, my dad called to say hello, and in the course of the conversation he disclosed weekend plans to watch a Little League baseball game in a neighboring town.

"Who's playing?" I asked.

"The nephew of a guy who works in the same building as your mom's first cousin," he said.

"Sounds too good to miss," I answered and made plans to meet him there.

The next Saturday, we were sitting in the bleachers before the game, watching the players warm up.

"Here comes the shortstop," my dad said.

"How do you know?" I asked.

"Saw him sneaking a butt in the parking lot when I got here," he said.

"There's the third baseman," I added, pointing to a kid with grass stains and mud blotches on his uniform.

A car stopped on the road and a tall kid jumped out and jogged across the outfield. He ran effortlessly with long strides; his upper body never bobbed or bounced. We looked at each other and said simultaneously, "Center fielder."

In rapid succession we alternated identifying players on both teams, noticing the same clues, agreeing with each other on every pick. On one team, the pitcher was combing his hair and the catcher was scratching his crotch. During the national anthem, the second baseman stood at attention with his hat over his heart. The right fielder stood by himself until the first baseman walked by and knocked the outfielder's cap off while the left fielder strolled behind the backstop collecting buttercups.

On the other side of the field, the pitcher was talking to two giggling girls, the left fielder was the only player without a baseball glove, the second baseman was having his picture taken with the batboy, and the center fielder was balancing a bat on the tip of his nose.

A heavyset woman arrived carrying a plate of cookies in one hand and dragging the right fielder with the other. We identified the third baseman when she called, "Hi, Sonny," to a boy trying with little success to tie his shoelaces. We guessed the rotund one was the catcher even before he started to put on his chest protector. One kid was on the mound throwing fastballs to a skinny kid behind the plate, who dove to his left to snare a wild pitch.

"Shortstop, I figure," my dad said of the latter, adding, "I knew it!" when the kid's return throw sailed five feet over the head of his teammate.

"First baseman's the kid on the mound," I said.

"I don't see that one," he challenged. "Prove it."

"He keeps looking over at the coach to see if he's watching and the coach is ignoring him. He's a wannabe and the first baseman always wants to pitch."

"Good call," Dad conceded.

This was an old contest we played based on our observations of hundreds of similar youth baseball games. It allowed us to define and refine our philosophy. We took turns making our picks, scoring a point for every correct selection and subtracting a point for every wrong one. A challenge doubled the value.

When the teams took the field we both had nine correct picks, but I was up by a point due to his challenge.

"Let's do the crowd," he urged, hoping to rally in the ninth and send the game into extra innings.

Spectators are harder because the only way to settle a dispute is to ask the onlooker what position he used to play. Since neither of us liked approaching strangers to pose the question, our rule is whoever challenges has to do the asking.

We scanned the crowd of adults, picking the obvious ones. Both of us knew that coaches who selected their sons to pitch had been first basemen, guys who keep score books, second basemen, and dads who watched everything but the game were left fielders. My dad nailed me by identifying a former pitcher by his gold cuff links and silk shirt, but I countered with an ex-shortstop who arrived on a motorcycle.

It wasn't a big crowd and we had identified all the gimmes when Dad tagged an off-duty cop as a third baseman. I watched him for a while and wasn't certain. He had no beer belly for one thing, and his shoes had a pretty good shine for another. I challenged.

The game was over and the crowd was dispersing but I followed the cop to the parking lot where he climbed into a pickup truck. I knew right away I had struck out, even before noticing the "Honk If I Love Baseball" bumper sticker.

"You win," I reluctantly admitted. "How did you know?"

"Saw him over at the refreshment stand," Dad said. "Guy asked him if he took mustard and relish on his hot dogs and he said, 'I don't know, I'll have to check with my wife.'"

"So you knew from the get-go and saved him until the end, huh? Nice job. The shine on the shoes threw me off."

"They're plastic-covered perpetual-shine shoes," he said. "They gave me a double take, too."

Before splitting up, we stopped for dinner at a place called T.J.'s Sports Bar in Northampton, Massachusetts. We selected a table beneath a photograph of Ted Williams and continued to play our game with the bar's clientele.

We were circling topics close to the heart the way dogs circle hydrants, but finally our conversation turned to personal matters, like each other's health, the activities of other family members, and the baseball strike.

I described the empty pit in my stomach, the crawling skin, the tremors, my social ineptness and unemployability. He nodded, fully understanding. He started to relate sleepless nights, temper tantrums, and spiritual despair when I interrupted him.

"Dad," I said, "you're crying."

He had always tried to be strong in front of me. To that day, I had seen him cry only three times: when Yaz retired, when the ball squirmed between Buckner's legs, and when I accidentally dropped a shovel on his little toe. That day, it must have been the combination of seeing a game, sitting under a picture of the Splendid Splinter, and talking to a kindred soul that just got to him. The floodgates opened. He cried like the time I crushed his pinky toe.

I stammered, "I know how you feel, Dad," and then began sobbing right along with him. There we were, tears flowing, bodies trembling, unable to console each other, crying without shame or embarrassment in a public restaurant. The waitress thought somebody died, and she ran to fetch the owner.

"What is it?" the owner asked. "The food? Too well done? Too much garlic?"

Neither of us could find our voices. We just shook our heads no.

He picked up our bill and looked at it. "Is it my prices?" he wondered. "Three bucks for a burger too heavy for you big spenders?"

We were out of control. Both of us folded our arms on the table and buried our faces on them.

"Were you guys second basemen?" he asked.

We both nodded yes.

The owner turned to the waitress. "It's the strike," he said. "I don't know why, but it affects second basemen like this. Leave them alone and they'll get over it after a couple beers."

When we were composed, the owner returned with a complimentary beer and sat down with us. His name was John Smith and he was very kind and consoling but unable to understand our misery.

"What is it with you second basemen?" he asked. "Don't you have real lives? Is baseball that important?"

We tried to explain, but John Smith could not comprehend the depth of our feeling for the grand old game. As we talked, the truth sank in: It is impossible to understand the agony of cold-turkey withdrawal from baseball unless you played the keystone sack. We were very good at noticing how playing a particular position affected others but not so perceptive at seeing how completely second base had molded us. Baseballism, we realized for the first time, is a disease peculiar to second basemen.

It was all alien to John Smith.

"I don't get it," he admitted.

"That's because you never played second base. Hell, you never even played baseball," my dad said.

"How'd you know that?" he asked.

"Because you own a sports bar," I told him.

We proceeded to explain our theory of how baseball affects adolescents and how the position they played determines personality. "It's a combination of the importance society puts on the game, the intensity of the experience, and the impressionability of children," I explained.

"You guys oughta write a book," John Smith said as he stood up and walked away.

"We should," Dad agreed, "but we'll be giving up our edge if we reveal our theory to the world."

"Yeah, but what good is having an ace in the hole after the game is over?" I asked.

"Maybe," Dad said wistfully, "if we convince everyone of baseball's role in shaping the personalities of the kids who play it, the owners and players will come to their senses and reach an agreement to end strikes and lockouts forever."

With that hope in mind, we present to the world this explanation of the Ryan Theory of Adolescent Development in American Males.

3

The Importance of Baseball

Next to religion, baseball has furnished a greater impact on American life than any other institution.   —*Herbert Hoover*

When you're playing for the championship, it's not a matter of life or death. It's more important than that.   —*Duffy Daugherty*

Some people, even some very perceptive, intelligent, and insightful people, people of standing in the community and distinction in their fields, say baseball is a game. This is a lie. It's not false because the statement is untrue, but because the statement is incomplete. Because it isn't the whole story, it's deceptive.

It's like saying the Sahara Desert is a sand pit; the moon is a rock; the Amazon is a river; the Bible is a book; Babe Ruth was a baseball player; Reggie Jackson was a career .262 hitter. These statements may be true, but they're false just the same, because they fail to tell the whole story.

People who say baseball is a game always follow up the lie by asking, "How can anyone enjoy watching grown men play a little boys' game?"

That's a trick question, as unanswerable as "When did you

stop beating your wife?" Baseball is not a little boys' game. It's a game of grown men. A better question would be, "How can anyone enjoy watching little kids play a grown men's game?"

Little boys are not old enough, big enough, tough enough, or strong enough to play baseball the proper way, and there probably should be a law forbidding children to play organized baseball before puberty. Pickup games in farm fields, school yards, or sandlots or stickball in city streets or alleys, that's okay, but nine-on-nine games on lined diamonds with players in uniforms, coaches at the bases, managers on the sidelines, and spectators in the stands? That's too dangerous for children. Broken limbs are not the concern; it's broken hearts, wounded psyches, ruined lives. Baseball can be cruel, even to adults. Just ask Bill Buckner.

All cultures have taboos against children participating in some adult activities. In ours, a person has to be twenty-one to drink alcohol, eighteen to smoke cigarettes or join the army, seventeen to see a movie with frontal nudity or excessive violence, and sixteen to drive a car, work in a factory, or get married. We don't let eight-year-olds play with guns, why do we let them play organized baseball?

To many folks, this proposal might sound like something from left field. Not so. Based on the Ryan Theory, which has now been supported by interviews, polls, surveys, and research, organized baseball is the single most important influence on an American male's development and, as often as not, the effects are negative and permanent. To prove this concept, it must first be conclusively demonstrated that

BASEBALL AIN'T JUST A GAME!

Baseball has been called our national pastime, the American game, the national game. Presidents stop whatever else they are doing to start it; poets glorify and lament it; songwriters celebrate

20

it; philosophers explain it; historians record it; politicians evoke it; Hollywood glamorizes it. Advertisers use baseball to sell; preachers use it to moralize; writers use it to symbolize; educators use it to teach; mathematicians use it to demonstrate; parents use it to reward and punish; generations use it to bond. No game could do all that.

Baseball is the defining American experience. Its impact spreads from ball fields and stadiums to every nook and corner of American life. Columnist George Will blames his disposition (cranky) and political philosophy (conservative) on his youthful love for the perpetually cellar-dwelling Chicago Cubs. In the early part of this century, W. E. B. Du Bois urged blacks to organize teams as a way to achieve equality in America. Sociologists have credited baseball with helping to knock down the barriers faced by Irish, German, Italian, Polish, and other Eastern European immigrants. You can't hate a man who drives in the winning run for the old home team.

Poet Don Hall views baseball as "something in the world that I can count on and it will never let me down." That from a man whose favorite team plays its home games in Fenway Park! Historian Doris Kearns Goodwin, daughter of a die-hard Brooklyn Dodgers fan, avers that baseball is a connection between her dad and her children though her father died before they were born. Writer George Plimpton says it's the "deepest part of the American psyche." Mark Twain described baseball as the perfect symbol of America; in *Leaves of Grass*, Walt Whitman proclaimed baseball "glorious."

Writer Gerald Early claims that in two thousand years American civilization will be remembered for only three things: the Constitution, blues, and baseball.

A few examples should be enough to demonstrate the pervasive impact baseball has had on American culture.

First, let's dispel the myth that "The Star-Spangled Banner" is sung before each baseball game because it is the national anthem. The reality is that "The Star-Spangled Banner" is the national anthem because it is sung before each baseball game.

In 1918, the Boston Red Sox played the Chicago Cubs in the World Series. World War I was winding down and America was teeming with patriotic fervor. During the seventh-inning stretch of game one of the series, the band in Comiskey Park struck up "The Star-Spangled Banner." The fans joined the singing with gusto and broke into sustained applause after "the home of the brave." There was such whooping and hurrahing that the song was played during the seventh-inning stretch of each game in the series.

When the new season began in 1919, every major league game began with the crowd singing "The Star-Spangled Banner." So popular was the song, so strong were the feelings it evoked, that Congress was flooded with petitions to adopt it as the national anthem. After several years of grassroots advocacy, in 1931 Congress did so.

Baseball has transformed the English language by introducing hundreds of idiomatic expressions which refer to events, rules, or situations that occur in baseball games. Entire books have been written on this subject. Common expressions such as "out in left field," "off the wall," "home run," "in the on deck circle," "batting cleanup," and many more are immediately understood by all Americans but confusing to all other English-speaking people. In fact, lexicologists have determined that baseball terminology is the primary distinction between American and English speech.

Baseball terms have such universal acceptance in this country that they have transcended the category of slang and are frequently used in the highest social and professional circles. For example, throughout the country, legislative bills to enhance the prison sentences of repeat offenders are called "Three Strikes and You're Out" laws. Only a people immersed in baseball lore would understand this description.

In World War II, baseball expressions were used as passwords by American soldiers; the landing of men on the moon in 1969 was originally scheduled to coincide with the All-Star break to ensure citizen interest. Some political pundits have postulated that the "Angry Man" expulsion of incumbents from Congress in 1994 was fueled by the players' strike and the cancellation of the World Series.

Every American president since William Howard Taft has neglected his official duties to throw out the first pitch of the major league baseball season. In Boston so many employees call in sick for the Red Sox opener that the illness has a name—"Fenway Fever"—and it is an acceptable excuse for absence from work. In 1986, a worker fired for calling in sick on opening day sued his employer and the jury awarded him $1.3 million in punitive damages plus reinstatement and back pay.

An American man's character is evaluated and defined in baseball terms. "Don't die on third" is an exhortation to keep trying when close to a goal and tempted to quit. People asked to make a sacrifice are urged to "take one for the team." A man with "a good eye" shows sound judgment while one who "can't tell a ball from a strike" is a fool. Those graduating from school or starting new jobs, businesses, or any other enterprise are encouraged to "swing for the fences" or "hit one out of the park." After a disappointment, people are told to "dust yourself off and get back in the batter's box." Perseverance is judged by what one does with his "last at bat." In any critical situation in a man's life, those close to him will use baseball lingo to encourage, console, congratulate, or criticize.

Even an adolescent's sexual awakening will be measured by a baseball ruler. Every junior high school student in America knows what first base, second base, third base, and home mean when asked after a date, "How far did you get?"

Baseball also has a spiritual dimension to many Americans. Doris Kearns Goodwin finds in it "a promise of eternal life." Don

Hall sees a ballpark as "a place where memory gathers." George Plimpton denies that baseball is just a pastime. "It has to do with the spirit of the people," he says. George Will sees in it "a metaphor for life." Actor Billy Crystal marvels at its "mythical contradictions."

Branch Rickey, the man who integrated the major leagues, claimed, "Baseball has graced our country." Bob Costas puts baseball on the same level as family when he says without embarrassment, "It's one of the few things in my life I've cared about all my life." According to Studs Terkel, "Baseball has the same sense of peace as a church." Mario Cuomo has described baseball in terms of American democracy and declares the one reflects all that is good and decent in the other.

So, clearly, baseball ain't just a game. It's one part religion, one part culture, and one part philosophy, and all the parts are American red, white, and blue. To paraphrase the greatest of all American philosophers, Pogo, "We has met the game and baseball is us."

Now for the other shoe: BASEBALL AIN'T FOR KIDS!

4

Baseball Ain't for Kids

Whoever wants to know the heart and mind of America had better learn baseball.   —*Jacques Barzun*

Baseball is like Church. Many attend but few understand.
                                                        —*Wes Westrum*

Since baseball is so important, it's obviously much too serious for kids, and they should not be permitted to play it in their formative years. The introduction of young people to baseball should be gradual. Years of study should precede participation in organized leagues. Instead of banning baseball cards from classrooms, they should be an essential part of the curriculum, text for instruction in the grand old game. The core subjects of elementary education should be reading, 'riting, 'rithmetic, and baseball, not necessarily in that order. Under our present system, young children are suffering serious impairment to their self-esteem, moral development, and personal growth. Whose fault is this?

There's plenty of blame to go around. Parents set a bad example. A lot of them, particularly the father kind, buy mitts instead of pillows for the kids' cribs. Baseball writer Bill Geist reports that one man of his acquaintance used to put a portable radio on his wife's stomach while she was pregnant so the in utero short-stop could listen to Mets games. These dads expect their sons to live their dreams. Most of them were first basemen in their youth.

Kids themselves see grown men playing the game and try to imitate them without knowing the dangers. Where are the parents when kids take these risks? Children need supervision and direction or they find all sorts of perils. It must be impressed upon them that some of life's pleasures, like sex and baseball, are reserved for adults. Better they spend the quiet hours of childhood watching cable television and playing violent video games. It's healthier for the young to fill their little heads with images of pillage, rampage, and gore than dreams of double plays, home runs, and no hitters.

Our whole society pushes kids to grow up too fast—with boy-girl parties, lipstick on preteens, proms for eighth-graders, and batting gloves for ten-year-olds. The plague of teen pregnancies in the eighties was caused by boys who watched Wade Boggs swat doubles off the wall. Soon as those kids reached second base on a botched pop-up, they thought they were ready for Margo.

This problem appears in every generation. When Babe Ruth played ball for the Red Sox in staid old, puritan Boston, Victorian mores were the norm in America. As soon as he was sold to the Yankees and started chasing New York showgirls, debauchery and decadence spread like wildfire across the land. That's what caused the Roaring Twenties.

The baby boomers were only mildly curious about the opposite sex until Joe DiMaggio married Marilyn Monroe. They all had Yankee Clipper bats, Yankee Clipper gloves, and dammit, as soon as Joe tied the knot, they all wanted girlfriends with red lips, wide hips, and cleavage. In the sixties, Bo Belinsky set the bad example with Mamie Van Doren. In the nineties, we have Jose Canseco messing around with Madonna.

Roger Angell, lamenting Pete Rose's banishment from baseball, noted that we have "unrealistic expectations of baseball players." These expectations are not confined to the professionals; we place unreasonable and unfair hopes on our youngest players, too.

Given the exalted position of baseball in our culture, it should come as no surprise that a child's first experience in organized baseball is the defining experience of his life. That is the essence of the Ryan Theory of Adolescent Development in American Males and bears repeating:

> A child's first experience in organized baseball is the defining experience of his life.

How does this happen?

A child comes to youth baseball as raw, wet clay. He has not yet developed a self-image, a self-identity, or much of a personality. Society has not passed judgment on him; he has never been compared to his age peers; he has never stood in the public spotlight to be analyzed by friends, family, and strangers. Such a youth is a plowed field waiting for seeds of self-esteem to be planted, and he has had no preparation for what awaits.

Before his first season is complete, this child of seven or eight years will be appraised, assessed, tested, and judged. The clay of his personality will be packed into one of nine specific molds, baked in the furnace of public opinion and hardened into a permanent shape.

Whoever he becomes in his first year of baseball, he will be all his life. His character will be set in concrete. His role in life will be firmly determined. The range of his self-esteem will be unequivocally fixed. In his own eyes and in the eyes of the world, he can never be any more, nor any less, than what he was in his first year of baseball.

Here's how it happens. Psychologists tell us the brain is soft mush, pliable and pliant, sensitive to pressure. Every experience produces an impression on the brain, and the more intense the experience, the deeper the impression and the longer it lasts. A baby's brain starts off as smooth as its bottom, as unblemished as a raked pregame infield. No dents, no indentations, no cracks, no craters. Eventually, life turns it into the dark side of the moon, with more lines than the map of Manhattan, more wrinkles than George Burns, and more holes than the '63 Mets infield. Nevertheless, before baseball, an eight-year-old's cranium is smooth as Ken Griffey Jr.'s swing.

Now put this kid on an organized baseball team for a couple months in the summer. Remember, this isn't just a game he's playing. It's religion, culture, and country all rolled into one. We call each side a team but it's more a network of individuals with a common goal. In baseball, every player is on his own.

You can have the next Ozzie Smith at shortstop but if the ball is hit to third base he can't do a darn thing about it. The third baseman has to handle it alone. It's even worse at the plate. Your number three hitter might be putting up Frank Thomas–like numbers, but he can only cross his fingers and pray when the left fielder's at the plate with the game on the line.

To step into the batter's box is to be alone, isolated in the spotlight, naked under the watchful eyes of family, teammates, coaches, and spectators. Failure here is greeted by the rancor of friends and the ridicule of foes. When the first baseman goes down swinging for the fence with two on, two out, and his team down one, he trudges back to his bench to a chorus of Bronx cheers from his team and a stream of curses from his coach. What can he say? "Hey, it wasn't me. It was the shortstop who swung at that pitch." Nope. He's got to swallow it. In baseball, you can't pass the buck.

Suppose, on the other hand, the kid raps a single between shortstop and third. Two runs score and he's a hero. He comes home to high-fives, backslaps, hurrahs and hallelujahs, proud parents, and clapping fans. Everybody knows his name and he made his whole world happy. He may never again be so loved and appreciated. It's a tough life when you peak at age eight.

This happens only in baseball. In every other team sport there's shared responsibility. Baseball is a lonely sport, especially when it comes to blame, shame, and guilt. And no one forgets the goats. Just ask Mitch Williams or Stan Belinda.

"Baseball is intensely remembered," Roger Angell observes, "because only baseball is so intensely watched. The game forces intensity upon us." It is a combination of action and inaction, and between each event there is sufficient time for contemplation, cogitation, reflection, and memory formation by both the participants and the spectators.

What effect does a season of errors in the field and strikeouts at the plate have on a kid's pristine brain? Or a season of home runs, no-hitters, flawless fielding, and perfect throws? Or, as usually happens, a season mixed with triumphs and failures?

It carves a memory canal from the scalp to the teeth. You can K Tony Gwynn before you can erase the effects of that first year of baseball. Nothing the kid has ever done before will be as traumatic or dramatic, nor as public, pivotal, or profound. It's the combination of the cultural significance of baseball, the impressionability of young players, and the intensity of the experiences.

And the consequences are as predictable as high tides, sunsets, and Red Sox disasters. It all depends into which molds the youth baseball coach (YBC) loads the little urchins assigned to his care by trusting parents.

The molds into which the raw personalities of youthful players are poured are called positions. There are nine different molds; each forms distinct traits and each produces a unique personality type. The selection process is sometimes capricious but never random. Every choice has a logical, though sometimes erroneous, rationale. The decision maker is neither cruel nor compassionate, usually unbiased, and completely unaware of his omnipotence. Not that awareness would matter. The decision maker is the YBC and his decisions are motivated by the ambition to win. This is American baseball; every other consideration is secondary to victory.

These are the personality molds to which the YBC assigns his players for the rest of their lives:

1. Pitcher
2. Catcher
3. First Base
4. Second Base
5. Third Base
6. Shortstop
7. Left Field
8. Center Field
9. Right Field

The next step to understanding why baseball ain't for kids is to look at the raw material that is placed in each mold, the shape of the mold itself, and the finished product the mold produces. It doesn't matter who the YBC is or how pure his intentions are. He has so many kids and only so many molds. Every kid has to be put somewhere.

Every YBC follows the same selection process, beginning with the pitcher—who is the most important—and then down the line until the last kid is left. He's the right fielder. He's the least important player and the only reason he gets to play at all is that if the YBC doesn't field nine players, he forfeits, and a forfeit is a loss, and this is America.

5

The Pitcher

My only regret in life is that I can't sit in the stands and watch me pitch.
—*Bo Belinsky*

The Ingredients

On every youth baseball team, the most important player is the pitcher. He is the key to the team's success and a YBC cannot win without a good pitcher. Pitchers are thus the first player chosen on every team. Those chosen, in every instance, have a father who habitually played catch with them. Often is not often enough. The father must have taught, trained, and drilled the future pitcher like a Spartan soldier. In nine out of ten cases, the father was a first baseman.

Training is essential because there are no natural pitchers. The movement, consisting of the stance, the windup, the pivot, the leg lift, the stride, the release, and the follow through, is as complex as the Sunday *Times* crossword puzzle, and the percentages of

31

people who can complete either are equally minuscule. It takes hours of practice just to keep from falling off the rubber during the weight shift from the windup to the pivot.

The pitcher needs to be able to throw the ball accurately most of the time. This, too, takes practice. Ironically, speed, while an asset, is not a primary concern. No matter how slow a kid throws, at least four of the players on the other team will strike out every time they come to the plate unless they are walked or hit by a pitch. Even the best of the rest will be out twice as often as they hit safely. The two keys to pitching success in youth baseball are (1) avoiding walks and (2) beaning only the good hitters. This requires accuracy, and moderate speed will suffice.

Many children can throw the ball fast but few can throw it where they want it to go. Even if they are naturally talented, consistently hitting an intended target requires of them hours and hours of rehearsal. This can be acquired by throwing the ball against a wall, but baseball, like sex, lacks its special appeal without a second participant. This explains why the kid chosen as the team pitcher must always have a father who played catch with him from the time he could walk. Older brothers don't count. They want to pitch, so they make the younger brother catch. Mothers don't count. A kid who plays catch with his mother doesn't raise his elbow over his shoulder when he throws so he has to play right field.

Body image is important in choosing a pitcher. He cannot be short; he cannot be fat. He cannot be too tall or too muscular in comparison to other players in the league. The duel between pitcher and batter is a physical, emotional, and psychological battle. If the pitcher is too overpowering in size or physique, the spectators will taunt him unmercifully, suggesting he is too old for the league. Umpires will demand to see his birth certificate every time he goes to the mound.

Eight-year-olds do not have the self-confidence to withstand bombasts of criticism from angry adults or challenges to their legality and legitimacy by authority figures. Oversized kids have to play center field, where they will look smaller.

Much of the spectators' attention will be focused on the pitcher during the game, so he should have pleasant features. He will be the team leader but dependent on the support of his teammates. Kids will neither follow nor support a kid who is ugly. Also, the better looking a pitcher is, the more close calls he will get from the umpire. Human beings naturally favor attractive people; this is unfair but it's a fact of life, and YBCs instinctively know it.

The pitcher cannot, however, be so appealing to the eye that he can be characterized as a "pretty boy." Baseball is a macho game—that's why all the players spit—and if the pitcher is a pretty boy, the whole team will be dismissed as sissies. This label destroys team morale and disturbs the pitcher's concentration. The sissy taunt provokes the pitcher to throw harder, which compromises his accuracy and leads to walks.

YBCs, however, do not want pitchers who are accurate all of the time, just most of the time. It's good to drill an opposing player now and then, particularly numbers one and four in the order, since they are the most likely to reach base safely anyway. If there is a lesson to be learned from the career of the late, great Don Drysdale, it's that an occasional plunked batsman produces a healthy respect that ranges anywhere from polite deference to absolute dread.

Cracking the helmet of a batter with an inside fastball produces a base runner, but it's an investment in the future. The next few batters will strike out trying to hit from the on deck circle. Another plus is that after the ambulance leaves the field, no one ever calls the pitcher a sissy again.

After accuracy, body shape, and rugged handsomeness, the YBC wants his pitcher to have speed, but speed, like accuracy, can be overrated. If the pitcher is too fast, the catcher can't catch the ball. He'll hold up his mitt like a shield, close his eyes, and turn his head sideways. After the catcher hears the umpire call "ball" or "strike," he'll open his eyes, run to the backstop, retrieve the ball, and throw it back to the pitcher. This wastes much time, the ump's patience, and the catcher's arm. Hence, the best pitchers are fast but not scary-fast.

In summary, YBCs choose their pitchers first. Those chosen have a close, almost symbiotic relationship with their fathers, throw fast but not too fast, accurately, consistently, and wildly occasionally. They are tall but not too tall, solid but not fat, handsome but not pretty.

At first glance, it appears to be not only a critical decision, but a perplexing one. Not so. In most cases, it's the YBC's easiest call. He lines up all the kids on the team and gives every one of them a fair shot to be the keeper of the rosin bag. He checks form, motion, size, appearance, mechanics, and speed, noting his observations on a clipboard.

When the choice is narrowed to three wannabes, the YBC has them each pitch a batting practice; he checks fielding skills and evaluates leadership potential. He consults the assistant coaches and then does what everybody on the team knew he would do from the get-go: he makes one of the finalists his center fielder, another his first baseman, and then, without bias or favoritism, he selects his son as the pitcher. Nothing could be fairer. The team's destiny now rides on the arm of his heir and namesake.

The Mold

The development of pitchers apes the development of baseball as a game. In the early years of baseball, pitchers were the least important players on the field. They were called feeders and their role was to toss the ball underhand to the batters so they could try to hit it past the fielders. There was no limit to strikes and no base on balls. Hitters kept swinging until they connected. The first intercollegiate game was played under these rules on July 11, 1859, in Pittsfield, Massachusetts. Amherst College defeated arch-rival Williams, 66–32, establishing a tradition of lopsided Amherst victories that continues to this day.

We see this level of pitching when moms and dads play family baseball with their still-in-diapers firstborn son. The toddler wields a plastic bat as big as himself. While one parent patiently lobs the tyke beach balls, the other patiently videotapes the action until the kid blasts one into the living room lamp. The film is then filed away in the family archives in the hopes it will fetch millions at auction when the lad wins the Triple Crown.

When the New York Knickerbockers codified the first rules of baseball in the 1840s, they included the concept of balls and strikes. During the next eighty years, baseball was a pitcher's game. Hurlers like James Creighton, Albert Spaulding, and "Three Fingers" Brown dominated the sport and became its biggest stars. During this so-called "Dead Ball Era," Cy Young won 511 games and Walter Johnson threw 110 shutouts. These pitching records, in addition to many others set during the period, will never be rivaled, equaled, or broken.

Babe Ruth changed all that, but not until the 1920s. His popularity was so immense and he brought such a following to the game that the owners instituted rule changes to favor the long-ball hitter. They also approved changes in the composition and manufacturing of baseballs to make them livelier.

In a sense, organized youth baseball is a throwback to the Dead Ball Era when pitchers were the central players and their performances determined the outcome of games.

At the first level of organized youth baseball, twenty of the game's forty-two outs—seven-inning games are played—will be strikeouts. Each pitcher will strike out ten batters. This occurs so often, it might as well be a rule of the game. A few players can field, a fewer number can accurately throw to first base, but no one on the team except the second baseman can do both consistently. Hence nearly every time a batter hits the ball, he will reach base safely, usually on an error.

Incidentally, all home runs at this level are Kodak home runs—the name comes from a famous commercial for Kodak film—where a combination of throwing and fielding errors permits advancement around the bases. Innings usually end when one of the last four batters in the order strikes out.

Based on extensive research, the other twenty-two outs in each game come as follows:

4 . . . . Pop-ups to the first and second basemen.

6 . . . . Unassisted force outs by first basemen (4) and second basemen (2).

6 . . . . Ground balls to second basemen (4) and pitchers (2) who throw the runners out at first base.

2 . . . . Spectacular catches by center fielders.

2 . . . . Heads-up plays by shortstops.

In addition, there are two mystery outs per game, one by each team. It is not uncommon for these outs to involve some activity by the third baseman or the left fielder but their irregular occurrence make them unpredictable. This is why they are called mystery outs. By the way, the catcher never effects an out in youth baseball and the right fielder is involved in only one out per season.

Since the pitcher will be solely responsible for half the defensive outs, he is guaranteed to be the hero of every game. If he can't strike people out, the inning, never mind the game, is eventually called for darkness. The team's hope for victory rides on the pitcher's arm. He is the focus of attention and center of affection. He gets most of the high-fives and slaps on the back from teammates, the handshakes from fans, the hugs from coaches, and the ink in the local paper.

He is never forced to shoulder the responsibility for a loss; there are too many other players who committed errors and are easier to blame. When he walks off the field, someone will take his glove for him, and while his team is at bat his arm will be covered with a lucky towel or a special jacket. If he gets on base, someone will run his warm-up jacket out to him to keep his arm from tightening up. This is the Jim Bouton Treatment, so called because Bouton was the first relief pitcher driven from the bullpen to the mound in a golf cart.

If the man on the mound puts a pitch in a batter's ear, which he will try to do from time to time, the shortstop and first baseman will protect him from retaliation. The pitcher will never have to bag the bats or pick up the bases after a practice or a game. He will always be afforded the first drink at the bubbler and the front seat of the van on the ride to away games.

The pitcher will not be expected to stand in line or wait for his turn. Throughout the season, his uniform will never be dirtied or grass-stained. He will not be expected to slide into second base or run out pop-ups to the infield. He will be excused from pregame exercises and laps around the field so he can throw warm-up pitches to his coach/dad.

The effects of the Jim Bouton Treatment are permanent.

The Finished Product

By the time the first season of baseball is over, the process of making the pitcher is complete and he can be removed from the mold. Even if he never pitches again, he will have the personality of a pitcher for the rest of his life. He is now and forever a prima donna. He is proud, vain, conceited, self-centered, and full of himself. He has an eternal sense that the rules do not apply to him. He is special, very special.

For the rest of his life, he will need attention, admiration, and adoration. He will expect and most often receive the first piece of cake, the biggest slice of pizza, and the last beer in the six-pack. Pretty girls will love him and plain girls will dream about him. Adults will open doors for him, figuratively and literally. Senior year in high school, he will be elected president of the student council and chosen the Boy Most Likely to Succeed.

Life will be gentle to the pitcher. There will always be someone there to clear bumps off his road, to shovel his walk, to drive him home, to pick up his tab, to soothe his pains, to make excuses for him. He will never be held accountable for his failures. He will marry the homecoming queen and when the marriage breaks up, she'll be blamed and he'll be forgiven. Men will seek his company and women his bed. Throughout his life, the only person whom he will ever truly love will be himself. He will go far on charm, he will never develop character. Incidentally, both Presidents Ronald Reagan and Franklin D. Roosevelt were pitchers when they played youth baseball.

The pitcher will be successful in his career. He will receive good job offers and rapid promotions. His confidence in himself will wear well, and he will be viewed by others as someone who gets things done, even though others do the grunt work. He will never get his hands dirty or have to wear a uniform to work. He will always be conscious of his appearance, dress fashionably, keep himself neat and well groomed.

Politically, he will always be a conservative and may even seek elective office. If he does, people will donate generously of their time and money to his campaign and he will win easily. He will, however, suffer greatly from public criticism and react meanly. Throughout the campaign he will appear aloof and above the fray, but behind the scenes he will have his opponent's reputation slandered, attacked, bloodied, muddied, and mangled.

Whomever opposes him in his ventures or pursuits he will view as evil, and he will seek through others to destroy him. He will never forget the feeling of power that surged through him after beaning a batter, and he will secretly delight in being feared.

Pitchers gravitate toward careers in the public eye. Hollywood is full of them. Seventy-two percent of television news anchormen were pitchers in youth baseball. Ditto for over half of the male models in a recent New York City survey. If pitchers start or buy their own business, they use their given name as the company title, adding an Inc. or Ltd., and they always appear in their company's television commercials. They name their firstborn sons after themselves, adding a III because most pitchers are Juniors to begin with.

Ex-pitchers have names for their primary residences and summer homes and they execute prenuptial agreements before each of their marriages. Each of their wives have feline names like Muffy, Buffy, or Kitty. They drive Mercedes SELs and BMW 3 Series, wear Rolex watches and engraved cuff links. Tennis, skiing the Alps, and polo are their post-baseball athletic interests.

If you attend a charity event that publishes a program, all the former pitchers in it will be listed as patrons. Sixty-five percent of the skippers competing for the America's Cup in 1990 began their athletic careers on the mound. Were it not for ex-pitchers, the company that manufactures Grecian Formula would be bankrupt and cosmetic surgery would be a poor man's business.

Pitchers are like politicians. All people detest them until they meet one face to face—then they are completely won over by their charm and social graces. They are experts at causing people, even their ex-wives, to love them.

If a former pitcher commits a crime, it's embezzlement or stock fraud. If he suffers from a chronic illness, it's gout; if he worships in a church, it's Episcopalian; if he sires more than two children, he will sire a minimum of eight.

Pitchers send their children to summer camps, private schools, dermatologists, orthodontists, and Ivy League colleges.

Whenever they order a cocktail, they specify the brand and it's always top shelf on the rocks with a twist or an olive.

Sometimes in life, it is necessary to know whether or not a person was a pitcher, but you don't feel comfortable being direct. No problem. You can always determine with reasonable certainty what position a suspect played by giving him the Jim Palmer test. This simple quiz works because the answer reveals values, interests, and intelligence and these are the keys to revealing position played. Just ask him what he remembers about Jim Palmer.

Answer	Position Played
A millionaire baseball player	Center Field
Earl Weaver's pain-in-the-ass pitcher	Shortstop
Rick Dempsey's battery mate	Catcher
Baltimore pitcher who got the calls	First Base
Orioles righty, ERA 2.86, 268 wins	Second Base
Invented Palmer Method of writing	Left Field
Name's Arnie and he played tennis	Right Field
I don't know	Third Base

If he breaks out in a wide grin and says, "Hurler with decent stuff, nicknamed Cakes, quit baseball to model Jockey underwear. The chicks loved 'im," as sure as God made green apples, the man was a pitcher.

6

The First Baseman

It's what you learn after you know it all that counts.   —*Earl Weaver*

George Bush was born on third base and thought he hit a triple.
                                                              —*Anne Richards*

The Ingredients

When the YBC selects his pitcher, he simultaneously selects his
first baseman, because the first baseman is the runner-up pitcher.
This is an automatic but very important decision. As was noted in
the previous chapter, strikeouts account for ten of the twenty-one
outs made by each team in a youth baseball game. Six outs per
game, over half of the remaining eleven, involve defensive participation by the first baseman. These rules are universal, as immuta-
ble as Newton's law of gravity. Either take our word for it or
examine the score books and box scores, as we did, of 781 youth
baseball games.

Three of these six outs will be unassisted. Twice a game, weak grounders from batters six, seven, or eight in the batting order—the late swingers—will be fielded cleanly by the first baseman who will tag his bag for the easy out. Once a game he will flawlessly glove a can of corn off the tip of the bat of hitter three or five.

The other three putouts will be two score-book four to threes (second to first) and a one to three (pitcher to first). That is, three hit balls will be fielded (two by the second baseman and one by the pitcher) and thrown, usually underhand in a soft lob, to the first baseman, who will manage to both catch the ball and keep his foot anchored on the bag. In addition, he will sometimes participate in the mystery out.

The value of the first baseman is now apparent. He accounts, individually or jointly, for almost 60 percent of the non-strikeout outs. No other fielder contributes so significantly to the speedy resolution of a youth baseball game. If the YBC has any hope of getting home before the nightly news, he needs an able and reliable first baseman.

The first baseman is tall, most often the tallest player in uniform. He is athletic and has good hands but is slow of foot. Otherwise, he would be the center fielder. Being able to catch requires that he have an older brother or involved father with a history of playing catch with him. It is sufficient if such play was an occasional occurrence. If it was habitual, his father would be the YBC and he would be the pitcher.

The first baseman is not afraid of baseballs hurled toward him as long as the ball speed does not exceed thirty miles an hour. He is willing to jump at balls thrown over his head and squat for balls thrown at his ankles. He must quickly learn to keep his heel or toe on the side of the bag. If he plants it in the middle, shortstops will instinctively target his lower leg and one will eventually break his ankle.

The first baseman is often a lefty because many of the major league first basemen are port siders and YBCs all think they are a phone call away from going to the Show. In the majors, lefties are first basemen because they don't have to pivot to throw to second and thus save 1.4 seconds on a double play ball. In youth baseball this means nothing because in its entire history, there has never been a 3-6-3 (first-short-first) double play.

The first baseman needs a decent arm because it's his responsibility to run infield drills while the pitcher is warming up and to start the ball "around the horn" after putouts. He needs to be able to concentrate because he must catch balls thrown to him while base runners approach him at full speed from another angle.

The first baseman is one of the four best athletes on the team, the others being the shortstop, center fielder, and pitcher. In the 87 percent of the cases where the pitcher's dad is the YBC, the first baseman is likely the best athlete on the team. If the team has two pitchers, he's the second starter. If the starter faces the ninth batter in the other team's order for the second time in any inning, the first baseman gets the call to relieve.

If the pitcher gets in trouble, it's the first baseman's responsibility to walk to the mound, talk kindly, and pat the pitcher on the butt. This is the universal sign of support in all levels of baseball, but in youth baseball only the first baseman has the stature to touch the pitcher's tush.

The first baseman is a surrogate pitcher, a frustrated pitcher, a could-have-been or should-have-been pitcher. He has one shortcoming that keeps him off the mound: as explained, the most common fault is that his father is not the YBC. In the other cases, compared to the real pitcher, he is too pretty or too plain, too fast or too slow, too consistent or too wild, or perhaps too tall. His one defect is minor. It's visible to the YBC but probably not to the first baseman and surely not to his mother, who asks after every game, "How come you didn't pitch today?"

The Mold

The first baseman is the pitcher's best friend as well as his chief rival. He loves him and hates him, supports him openly but wishes evils on him in his silent heart. Throughout the season, he is second best in every aspect of the game. He is the leader of the infield but not of the team. He accounts for the second largest number of defensive outs and the second fewest number of offensive outs.

In the local paper, the pitcher gets the headline and the first paragraph of the story; the first baseman's ink follows. When the game is won, the other players mob the pitcher, then slap the first baseman on the butt with a "Good game, man." His uniform seldom gets smudged with dirt but his shirt pulls loose from his pants when he leaps for high throws, and his socks slide down his calves and bunch at the ankles when he stretches for balls in the dirt.

Little girls swarm around him in the school yard but only to ask him if the pitcher likes anybody. Whatever way he answers, the girls giggle, "Well, I think he's cute," and run off hoping he'll pass on the message.

The first baseman has great responsibilities. It is his job to raise his fingers to indicate the number of outs every time a new batter comes to the plate. It is his job to start the infield chatter. If by some miracle the ninth batter on the other team reaches first base, it is his responsibility to execute the hidden ball trick.

When his team is at bat, it is his role to think of clever insults for the third baseman and catcher to yell at the other team's pitcher. It is his duty to call his infielders names when they make errors and to curse the left fielder for not paying attention. The first baseman is the team's enforcer. He must insist, in the interest of team morale, that nobody calls anyone but the right fielder an asshole.

The Finished Product

Being a first baseman in youth baseball is a death sentence. First basemen always develop ulcerated stomachs in their forties, have strokes in their fifties, and die of clogged arteries in their sixties. Pick an obituary from any newspaper in America and if the surviving family requests gifts to the Heart Fund in lieu of flowers, the deceased was a first baseman in his first year of organized baseball.

The common denominator of all first basemen is the ability to suppress seething anger and frustration while appearing calm and unruffled on the surface. By the time their first season is over, they will have come to believe in their heart of hearts that no matter how much they hustle, no matter how hard they work, no matter what the contest or race, they will always be second best. They will believe it but be incapable of accepting it. They will spend their whole lives seeking the answer to their mother's question, "How come you didn't pitch today?" and they will never find it. Nor will they ever be able to release their inner rage. It will eat them from the inside out until it kills them.

The first baseman lives his life in the pitcher's shadow or his reflected glory. When the pitcher marries, the first baseman will be the best man. When the pitcher produces offspring, he will be the kid's godfather. When the pitcher runs for elective office, he will be the campaign manager. The pitcher will call on him for support in difficult times and advice at critical times. The first baseman will keep a stiff upper lip and never say no to any request from the pitcher for fear of appearing jealous. He will take it like a man all his life.

Even in romance the first baseman will finish second. Though the first baseman will never trust his girlfriend when the pitcher is around, the pitcher will eventually steal her anyway. Pitchers just naturally believe that they have an inherent right to borrow whatever a first baseman possesses. First basemen have a learned feeling that whatever possessions they cherish will someday, somehow be purloined by the pitcher.

There will be only one time in his life that the first baseman will one-up the pitcher. When the pitcher's wife comes crying on his shoulder because the pitcher is ignoring her, the first baseman will end up in her arms and then her bed. His triumph will be sweet but short; pitchers always dump their first wives.

The first baseman will be a loyal ally to his infield mates but never consider any of them his equal. He will be condescending to third basemen and catchers, wary of shortstops, and impatient with second basemen. His deepest friendship will be with the center fielder, with whom he shares a common history. He will always be cruel to right fielders and antagonistic to left fielders, who are his complete opposite in temperament and philosophy.

The first baseman's political agenda will be right wing, promilitary, antitax, and antiwelfare. Even if he himself is gay or of color, he will oppose special considerations for minorities. Ex–first basemen make wonderful spies, being so experienced at wearing false faces. They bear up very well under torture and can fool polygraph machines.

George Bush and Clarence Thomas were both great athletes, the best on their teams, and both ended up first basemen. This explains why Bush was (1) such a great VP to President Reagan, (2) able to hoodwink the trusting second baseman/Boy Scout Michael Dukakis, and (3) guilty of underestimating right fielder Bill Clinton. It also explains the affinity between Bush and Thomas and the justice's bitterness and sour views.

Despite the first baseman's suppressed anxieties, his life will be judged highly successful by American standards. As second best, he's still in the top tenth percentile. He'll work hard and drive himself relentlessly to try and shake his inner doubts. In fact, he will often rise further in business, social status, and material wealth than the pitcher, but he will never feel equal to the man on the mound.

The first baseman will be a materialist who keeps score on his contemporaries. He will tend to judge others by the size of their stock portfolios, by the number of cars parked in their garages, by the square footage of their offices and homes. Employees who complain that someone else has a bigger office or better view are former first basemen. They pick their friends and associates on social status and prestige in the community, more on what they have than on who they are.

First basemen are frequently bullies. They find humor among their peers in racist and sexual jokes, even if their public conduct is exemplary, as it most often is. Many have a secret fondness for pornography. They will not be confrontational but will attack perceived enemies from behind screens or through surrogates. Their public images and private identities will be misaligned. The phrase "I should have . . ." will frequently crop up in their recounting of events.

First basemen will always be above average in height and intelligence and look down on short men and stupid people. They will not tolerate fools. They will be centers or power forwards on their high school basketball teams; enjoy golf but be plagued with putting woes; play competitive tennis but have trouble covering the court, making them desirable partners in doubles but embarrassingly beatable in singles.

First basemen will drive big black cars, wear black custom-made suits, keep black-handled .357 magnums in the chests by their beds, and have black Dobermans, Labrador retrievers, or cocker spaniels for family pets. Whenever a first baseman reseeds his lawn, hordes of black crows will feast on the bounty. He will have a fondness for black-and-white movies. This penchant for noir is a reflection of the seething, dark rage in their souls.

If there is a word to describe first basemen, it is *conventional*. All their likes, tastes, opinions, and convictions will be in the mainstream. All fads will be bizarre to them; movements anathema; causes a waste of time and energy. They will always speak of the good old days, listen to music from the big band era (Glenn Miller being a personal favorite), and keep a bookcase of the classics in their living room. Will Rogers will be their favorite comic, F. Scott Fitzgerald or Ernest Hemingway their favorite writer, and H. L. Mencken their favorite philosopher.

If a first baseman smokes, he will disdain cigarettes for pipes and an occasional cigar and will ask friends traveling to Mexico to bring him home a box of Cubans. Bourbons, scotches, and distilled whiskeys will be his libations of choice, the older the better, but he will take his alcohol in moderation. When his friends visit, he will barbecue steaks on his backyard grill and smother them with onions and his private-recipe sauce.

First basemen shave every day (even on vacation), polish their shoes, floss after every meal, see their dentist twice a year, their optometrist every second year, and their personal physician every June 15.

First basemen will all be pillars in their communities, upright and righteous citizens. Most, however, will cheat on their taxes, pad their expense accounts, and commit adultery when far from home. Twenty-three percent of those surveyed admitted to a secret fantasy of being spanked by a raven-haired, overweight dominatrix wearing a black bodice, black boots, and black mesh stockings held up by a black garter belt.

When the first baseman has children, he will name his first-born legitimate son after himself. All "Juniors" are the offspring of first basemen. This is a desperate attempt at a second chance. The first baseman will devote his life to protecting his namesake from the prejudices that scarred his soul.

Most YBCs were first basemen. Their sons will be pitchers, of that they will make certain. As soon as Junior can make a fist, he will have a ball in his fingers. Senior will hustle home from work to play catch with Junior; he will drill and train and prepare his second coming for youth baseball, not out of love, but out of vengeance. When the lad is old enough to play organized baseball, the father will be the YBC even if he has to sponsor the team.

And then a strange happening occurs. The first baseman mellows. He finds a sense of justice. He experiences a rebirth, a resurrection, and like a born-again Christian, he finds peace and balance. He will continue to live in the shadows and reflected glory of the pitcher, but this hurler will be his son. He will not be bitter or jealous and may, because of it, live a much longer and healthier life.

Let's take a last look at George Bush, our quintessential first baseman. In January 1991 he exited 1600 Pennsylvania Avenue a beaten man, runner-up again, a second-place finisher to a player he perceived as less qualified and deserving than himself. One of the worst moments of his political life was when Anne Richards, governor of Texas, described him as a man "born with a silver foot in his mouth."

In November 1994 George W. Bush defeated Anne Richards and was elected governor of Texas. George the daddy was born again, given a second chance at redemption and purged of his anger and frustration by his son, the pitcher, who carries his name. May his remaining days be spent in peaceful contemplation of white-lined green fields while he watches his son and namesake perform in the spotlight.

As for Anne Richards, well, shucks, she's a natural-born shortstop. Her joy comes from being in battle regardless of the outcome. As shown in the next chapter, so long as she can go down swinging, she could not care less who wins the fight.

7

The Shortstop

Sports do not build character. They reveal it.   —*Heywood Hale Broun*

Try to hate your opponent. Even if you are playing your grandmother,
try to beat her fifty to nothing.   —*Danny McGoorty*

The Ingredients

Some creatures on this planet cannot be disguised. Every living
person over the age of two knows a zebra, a whale, and a snake
when they see one. And everyone who knows baseball knows a
shortstop when they meet one.

Inch for inch, pound for pound, shortstops are the best baseball players in America. Their drawback is they have less inches
and fewer pounds than everybody else. But moxie? Guts? Feisti-
ness? Mouth? Shortstops have them all in royal flush spades.

Over half the entire team's spirit is crammed into the scrawny,
scrappy spitfire who stakes out the dirt between second and third
base. Shortstops are scary people. Given a choice of enemies
between the IRS, the FBI, and the Navy Seals on one hand and an

eight-year-old shortstop on the other, take your chances with the feds. If you insult a Mafia godfather and he sends his goons to slaughter your family, adopt a shortstop and you'll never lose a night's sleep.

The youth league board of directors puts a notice in the paper that team tryouts are on Saturday. Two hundred kids show up, all trying to impress the coaches with their own custom-made bats, Barry Bonds alligator-hide gloves, Cal Ripken cleats, and shiny white baseball pants. Fathers arrive with their high school championship jackets, offering to give the YBC a hand, and mothers appear in halter tops and short shorts volunteering to organize a pep club.

YBCs with clipboards bark out commands to line up in single file, and two hundred wannabes start pushing and shoving to be first in line. As order is restored, a snot-nosed runt in a tattered sweatshirt, torn dungarees, and black sneakers pedals his bike across the field with a butt in his mouth, a sneer on his lip, and a moth-eaten ratskin of a glove hanging from the handlebar. He drops the bike in the middle of the field, grabs his glove, smacks it a couple times, and walks to the front of the line. No one complains. Meet the shortstop.

This is the kid every YBC wants. As the prospects are graded in running, throwing, catching, and hitting, he'll receive mediocre scores and every YBC will note, "bad attitude" in the remarks section. When the selections are made, YBCs' sons, also known as pitchers, are automatically assigned to their dads' teams. Then the free-for-all begins. The mediocre kid with the bad attitude will be the first kid picked. Some YBCs have been known to deny their own sons' legitimacy to get the right shortstop. No son ever complained.

The shortstop is from a family of fourteen kids, and five of the six oldest are doing hard time; the other one is a priest. His father, if he has one, is a cop. For reasons that baffle modern science, whatever his racial background, he usually has red hair. He has never played baseball but his probation officer has ordered him to try out.

Fearful of his corrupting influence, parents forbid their children to play with the shortstop and shudder at the mention of his name. Despite such parental edicts, he is the most popular kid on the team. He's funny. Even the butts of his jokes can't help laughing at his insults. Don Rickles and Eddie Murphy started out as shortstops.

During the first practice, the shortstop gives everyone on the team a nickname that will stick for life. Often the nickname refers to a prominent feature of the player's anatomy and parents will cringe every time they hear it, but each kid will wear it like a badge.

At the end of practice the YBC will line the kids up on the third base line to run wind sprints to left field and back. The shortstop will beat everyone, even the center fielder, by ten yards. By the time the catcher finishes the race, the shortstop will be behind the bleachers dragging on another cigarette.

Shortstops are incorrigible, irrepressible, bold, and disrespectful. And everybody loves them.

The Mold

Two thirds of the ground balls hit in youth baseball will be to the pitcher's right. Most of the first five batters have the bat speed to get partially around on the ball; most of the last four strike out. Ninety percent of those ground balls will be stopped by the shortstop. The other 10 percent go to the third baseman and half of those will make it through to the outfield. Nothing gets by the shortstop.

The shortstop plays deep and has incredible range. Crouching as the ball travels to the plate, he is the picture of concentration. His first step is so quick camcorders capture only a blur. He dives, he jumps, he lunges, he charges. The only balls he ever misses are slow rollers hit right at him. These go through his legs like a croquet ball through wickets.

This occurs because he isn't challenged by balls hit right to him, and his battery isn't activated except by challenges. The harder the ball is hit, the quicker he reacts. The farther from him the ball travels, the more spectacular his fielding.

What he does with the ball after catching it or knocking it down is another story. The shortstop is a wild thrower. The first baseman hates to see him pluck the ball clean and set to throw the runner out; the ball is as likely to end up in the stands as it is in his glove. Sometimes it sails ten feet over his head into the dugout. Sometimes it beans the pitcher. No one ever knows. It's the challenge thing.

Like a dog pissing on hydrants, the shortstop stakes out his territory and dares anyone to try to get the ball past him. To the shortstop, fielding is a contest between him and the batter. It's like a Western gunfight. One against one. Mano a mano.

Throwing, on the other hand, requires collaboration between the thrower and the receiver. It's one to one, not one against one. To a shortstop, this is sissy stuff and he couldn't care less. No challenge = No concentration = No connection. As Tommy Heindrich explains, "Catching the ball is a pleasure. Knowing what to do with it is a business."

The wise YBC will eventually tell his shortstop not to throw to first base, just to hold the ball and run to second. This holds the runner at first. If he throws it, the runner will be safe at second, maybe third, and with a little luck and either another wild throw or a botched catch, the runner possibly will have a Kodak home run.

A shortstop's defensive value is not in effecting outs but in limiting runs by preventing extra-base hits. In most games he will effect only two outs but they will be on plays of such magnitude that they will be talked about only in superlatives.

The YBC's advice is accepted by the shortstop because it provides him with a double challenge. It's now him against the batter, then him against the runner at first. The next time the shortstop stops a grounder, he can race the runner from first to second, and if he wins, which he usually does, he not only has forced an out, but the luckless runner is right there by his side and he can jeer in his face. Shortstops, remember, are mouthy. Not only does the shortstop have the opportunity to talk a little trash, but if it's really his lucky day, the runner forced out will be mad enough to push him and the shortstop can then beat the crap out of him.

Shortstops love to fight. Give a shortstop a choice of a black eye or a home run and he'll go home with an eye swollen shut every time. A shortstop doesn't even care who wins the fight; his glory is in the process, not the result. He will happily take three or four shots in the head for every one he delivers. Fear of pain is not a deterrent; pain itself is of no consequence. Having anywhere from three to six older brothers, he is very much accustomed to beatings.

When a shortstop is fighting, either he wins or somebody breaks it up. This is a dangerous undertaking, and teammates (except for the second baseman) are reluctant to attempt it. Second basemen develop the knack of stepping in immediately after the shortstop has delivered an effective blow to the opponent, an ideal moment for cessation of hostilities from the shortstop's perspective, for it affords him the opportunity to admire his handiwork. Shortstops like to watch noses bleed and red abrasions turn purple.

The shortstop's lust for combat is usually limited to opponents who are twice his size, and he will never attack a teammate except in another's defense. All shortstops disdain bullies regardless of uniform color. To the weak and meek, shortstops are protectors. While it is permissible for them to razz and rank on anyone they choose, there is a gentle kindness to their taunting of right fielders, catchers, and third basemen in addition to anyone smaller or younger than themselves.

This instinct to protect others derives from being in the middle of a large brood of children where parental responsibilities are spread too thin for adequate supervision and the shortstop has to fend off his elder siblings and shield those younger. Deprived of meaningful relationships with Mom and Dad, shortstops yearn for attention and affection. The former they receive from combat with the mighty; the latter from defense of the vulnerable.

Shortstops are proficient in the art of infield chatter. While the second baseman chants support for the pitcher, the shortstop dumps on the batter. At this aspect of the game he excels. Most batters would sooner face a wild pitcher than a mouthy shortstop. A beanball only stings for a while; a sharp-tongued shortstop can label you for life.

A sixty-year-old bartender named Banjo Burns confessed he picked up his nickname when an opposing shortstop hollered he couldn't hit the ball with a banjo. When he proceeded to strike out, everyone—his teammates, his family, even his own mother—immediately embraced Banjo as his first name.

Obviously, shortstops have a common denominator, a distinguishing feature which sets them apart from the other kids on the team, indeed, from the rest of humanity. They're all a little bit crazy.

The Finished Product

James Dean, Lee Atwater, Richard Petty, and 86 percent of Congressional Medal of Honor winners played shortstop as kids. Only shortstops jump on grenades to save the team. A good rule of thumb is that if an adult male is described as "ruthless and reckless," he was a shortstop at eight years old.

Bobby Kennedy is a typical example. A middle child in a large family, he was renowned for challenging the powerful and defending the weak. He spent vacations white-water rafting and mountain climbing, loved to fight, and had a hard-earned, well deserved reputation for ruthlessness. Though he never weighed much over a hundred fifty pounds, he played college football and stayed in one game with a broken leg. If you were drafting a team, he'd be your number one pick.

Shortstops' futures are unpredictable; other factors and influences will dictate whether they end up in Sing-Sing or as CEO of a self-made Fortune 500 company. Many die young. They are wild and fearless and the years between fifteen and twenty-five are particularly perilous for them. Those adolescents who play chicken with cars, dive off railroad trestles, and walk on the ledges of skyscrapers are all shortstops.

Shortstops seldom stay in baseball for long but those that do flourish at the sport. Over half the men in the Hall of Fame started as shortstops, including Ty Cobb, Mickey Mantle, Carl Yastrzemski, and Don Drysdale. All the others, except for a wee smattering of catchers and pitchers, started as center fielders.

Most shortstops migrate toward more physical sports. In high school, they love to play football. If you go to a Thanksgiving Day game and see a 130-pound middle linebacker making unassisted tackles in the backfield, you know you're watching an erstwhile shortstop.

Rugby and lacrosse are also shortstops' favorites in places that offer such sports. Demolition derbies and stock car races would not exist without shortstop drivers. A survey conducted in the U.S. Army from 1967 to 1970 showed that while not all Airborne Rangers were former shortstops, all former shortstops were Airborne Rangers.

Shortstops are overrepresented in dangerous occupations. Those men who fly into the North Sea to put out fires on oil rigs are typically shortstops. Few, if any, enter the law enforcement field. Their natural sympathies lie with outlaws and underdogs.

Undercover work may have some appeal, but shortstops are not sly, shy, or deceptive. They loathe sneak attacks and backstabbing. When they come at you, they come head on, nose to nose. Shortstops frequently become union organizers and, whatever their profession, no former shortstop has ever been a scab or crossed a picket line.

Shortstops are steadfast in friendships and enjoy the absolute loyalty of countless comrades. Shortstops are known to appear from nowhere in times of crisis with an emergency loan, a bottle of scotch, a bouquet of flowers, or bail money. When your father dies, your wife leaves, your factory closes, or your car gets repossessed, the shortstop is there on your doorstep.

Shortstops' funerals are huge and the grief of surviving friends is long and profound. Every high school in America has a graduation award named for an alumnus who played varsity shortstop.

Shortstops are amorous, gallant, and horny. They love being loved and will have countless short romances throughout adolescence. Years later, the mere mention of their names will elicit tender smiles on the faces of their old flames. They relentlessly, indiscriminately, and unabashedly flirt even in the presence of their sweethearts. Age, status, appearance, and situation do not matter.

They test their charms and the limits of propriety on female state troopers, nuns, grandmothers, preschoolers, and meter maids in churches, elevators, hospital emergency rooms, bomb shelters, classrooms, courtrooms, and closets. Few shortstops grow taller than 5'9" but they have a decided preference for tall, big-breasted women and women in uniform. Whenever you see a man of average height escorting a woman over six feet tall, you're watching a former shortstop in action. It's the challenge thing, the going for what seems to be out of reach. Despite their natural and irrepressible flirting, shortstops, once committed to a relationship, are strictly monogamous.

Shortstops, though short, do not have the short man complex.

They are not little Napoleons. The world is full of little men who have a compulsion to prove their toughness, power, or strength. Shortstops don't have to prove anything. They are tough. They are powerful. They are strong. And everybody knows it.

There are only three certainties in life: death, taxes, and shortstops whom you will remember all your life and love with all your heart.

8

The Second Baseman

You spend a good deal of your life gripping a baseball and it turns out it was the other way around all the time.
—*Jim Bouton*

The Ingredients

In a perfect world, your car would start every morning, it would never rain on weekends, and love would last forever. Alas, reality is not so kind. Batteries run dead, golf matches are rained out, and love fades so fast and frequently that the whole world easily recognizes *true* love. Here's the total list: Romeo and Juliet, Anthony and Cleopatra, Frankie and Johnny, Tracy and Hepburn, Bogey and Bacall, second basemen and baseball.

When an eight-year-old kid shows up for youth baseball tryouts with six years of experience, he's a second baseman. His grandfather, for whom he was named, played second base for a Double A team forty years ago. The kid carries the picture in his pocket for good luck. He might even be using Grandpa's old glove, which he found in the attic covered with Saran Wrap.

The second baseman is a baseball trivia freak. He knows the stats of every current major league player and every Hall of Famer. He has memorized the box scores of every World Series game ever played, and can imitate the voices of Red Barber, Curt Gowdy, and Joe Garagiola. He idolizes some obscure second baseman, like Ted Lepcio or Jerry Remy, who no one else remembers, and he will argue knowledgeably and endlessly that his hero belongs in the Hall of Fame despite a mediocre reputation. The kid knows more baseball than the YBC and the only position he ever wants to play is second base.

Second basemen are not natural athletes but are born baseball players. Their abilities are mastered through hard work and single-minded devotion. They are the first kids to arrive at practice and the last to leave. As long as a YBC will pound out ground balls, the kid will field them. As long as someone will pitch to him, he'll swing the bat. If you drive by a baseball diamond an hour after sunset and hear a voice from the dark yelling, "Come on, come on, pitch me one more," you know it's a second baseman.

Second basemen are trustworthy, loyal, helpful, friendly, courteous, kind, obedient, cheerful, thrifty, brave, clean, and reverent. Boy Scouts. They do a good turn daily and are always prepared, particularly for baseball. Other parents love them. YBCs wish they had a whole team of second basemen. Other kids are slow to take to them, put off by what they see as brownnosing, suspicious of their "goody two-shoes" character, leery of their enthusiasm. By the end of the season, second basemen are respected and admired by their teammates because they are so genuine. There is nothing phony about a second baseman.

The chemistry between second basemen and shortstops is unique. Complete opposites in personality, they meld, blend, and fuse. No one can explain this. Second basemen pray; shortstops curse. Second basemen train; shortstops smoke, chew tobacco, and steal beer from their parents. Second basemen are cooperative; shortstops, competitive. Second basemen play hard but fair; shortstops, ferocious and dirty. Second basemen break up fights; shortstops pick them. Second basemen gratify YBCs; shortstops infuriate them. Second basemen call umpires "sir"; shortstops call them assholes. Second basemen are disciplined and dependable; shortstops, wild and incorrigible.

Yet somehow they bond for life. Second basemen provide shortstops stability; shortstops supply second basemen excitement. The only person who can convince the shortstop to mellow out or calm down is the second baseman. The only one who can crank up or piss off the second baseman is the shortstop. The second baseman is the only reason the shortstop ever practices; the shortstop is the only reason the second baseman ever does anything else.

Second basemen love playing baseball so much that winning is not their primary objective; just playing is enough for them. The only one who cares less about the score is the left fielder, who seldom even knows what it is. Second basemen have even been known to deliberately strike out or muff a grounder to send a game into extra innings. They show up to play or practice come hell, high water, or hurricanes, and their biggest fear is a rain cancellation. Cal Ripken Jr. may play shortstop now but he has the soul of a second baseman, and we'll eat his shorts if he didn't start his career as a keystone sacker. Even as adults, second basemen get more excited over the words "Play Ball!" than "Free Beer!"

The Mold

Second basemen are the most active players on the field. Though few balls come in their direction, they move on every play. If the ball goes to the outfield, they run to receive the relay. If the ball goes to the pitcher's right, they cover their own base. If it's a grounder to the first baseman, they try to cover his base. Whenever there is a runner at first, they cover their base after every pitch even if stealing is not allowed by the youth league rules. It's good training, they figure.

Whenever the other team makes an out with the bases empty, the second baseman demands the ball be whipped around the infield, even if no one can catch it. Second basemen love the feel of the ball in their hands. When no one is looking, they will lift the ball to their nostrils and breathe deeply. If you happen to see a kid kiss a baseball, you can be sure he plays second base.

While it's the first baseman's honor to start the infield chatter, it's the second baseman's prerogative to keep it going or change the chant. His chatter is all positive. The second baseman never tells an opposing hitter to "put a Band-Aid on that cut." That comes from the shortstop. You never hear a "Batter-batter-batter-batter, swing batter!" from the second baseman. It's all, "You-candoit-youcandoit-youcandoit, youdidit!"

While the first baseman is the player whose role it is to console the pitcher if things aren't going well, the second baseman is the first infielder there if the catcher or YBC goes to the mound. When the first baseman goes, it's to give support; when the YBC or catcher goes, the purpose is strategy and that's the second baseman's domain. After all, he knows how Cy Young, Walter Johnson, Sandy Koufax, Vida Blue, and Roger Clemens handled similar situations.

Second basemen do not have great quickness and that limits their range, but their gloves are like vacuum cleaners and their throws are always on target. Balls hit to them are automatic outs. Every move is almost mechanical, by the numbers and by the book. They get their bodies in front of the ball, watch it into the glove, and cover it with the throwing hand. They don't showboat. They don't hotdog. They never commit errors.

If they can get to it, they field it; if they field it, they deliver it. You know how the navy has those sonar missiles they can drop into a smokestack from a destroyer seven hundred miles away? The technology was developed studying the accuracy of eight-year-old second basemen gunning the ball to first.

In every game, the second baseman will participate in four outs. Once a game, he will field a ball close to his bag when there's a runner at first and step on second for the force. Only once a season will his throw to first arrive in time for the double play but he'll try for it every opportunity. Once a game a pop-up will come to his position. He will call for it, get under it, and catch it eye level with both hands exactly as Joe Morgan demonstrated to the kids on *The Baseball Bunch.* Twice a game he will shuffle, scoop, shoot to first, and beat the runner by a step.

It is unfortunate that so few balls are hit to the second baseman since he loves to field and never makes errors, but there are only twenty-one outs per side to go around.

One might ask why YBCs don't switch their shortstops and second basemen. Range is the answer. If the ball gets past the infield, the runner, unless he's a catcher, will be safe on at least second base. Unless there are two outs, any runner who hits a double will eventually score in youth baseball. Eight or nine balls a game will be hit toward the shortstop. He'll stop every one. He won't throw anyone out, but they will be held to a single as long as he doesn't try to throw anyone out. Singles don't hurt. If the second baseman was playing shortstop, he'd field the ball cleanly four or five out of the nine times and throw out the runner (or force an out at second by tagging the base) every time. The other four balls would be out of reach and go to the outfield, however, and the runner would reach second and score three out of four times. Range. That's why shortstops are shortstops and second basemen are second basemen.

The Finished Product

There are only two differences between second basemen at eight, eighteen, forty-eight, and eighty-eight. Size and shape. Their personality and character remain constant. They are Boy Scouts first, last, and always. Men of honor. Men who do their duty to God and to country and to whomever or whatever they serve.

You think marines are faithful and ready to serve, with their Semper Fi motto? They are fickle compared to second basemen. Moral men, who are described as "good and decent" all their lives, second basemen are oftentimes seen as too pure for the rough-and-tumble world they inhabit. You can bet your house Jimmy Carter played at the two-bag.

In their love lives, second basemen are polite, courteous, respectful, and willing to wait for marriage. Every mother wants her daughter to marry a second baseman, even if she herself prefers men with a little more pizzazz. Second basemen marry their childhood sweethearts, the girl next door, or the shortstop's sister. When they fall in love, they fall in love forever and if they don't marry their first honey, they never completely recover. If a woman is married to a second baseman, she should never let her husband go to his high school class reunion alone. He'll never leave her for a new love, only an old one.

The second baseman is an involved father. When you see a guy driving a station wagon, you know where he played the game. His backyard is the neighborhood playground and as often as not, he's right out there playing with the kids. He's more likely to have a baseball diamond than a swimming pool behind his house, and he mows his lawn and washes his car wearing the baseball cap of his favorite professional team. Of course, the primary game he plays with the kids is pickup baseball and his own kid is the second baseman, unless the boy has red hair. That's a sign he takes after his mother's side of the family and he'll be the short-stop. Scientists who study DNA have isolated a second baseman gene that is passed from generation to generation ad infinitum.

Professionally, second basemen are employers' dreams. They seldom go into business for themselves, preferring instead to be a part of a team. Many enter the social service occupations, becoming teachers, social workers, missionaries, or doctors. If they become lawyers, they will spend part of their careers as public prosecutors. If they are blue collar workers, they will be strong union men, but favor negotiation over agitation. They will always opt for cooperation over confrontation. They are natural peacemakers and peace lovers. Compelled by their love of country and patriotism, many will serve a stint in the armed services but none will make it a career, except as a medic or a chaplain.

Politically, second basemen are social liberals but fiscal conservatives. They believe strongly in volunteering and tithing to their church or general charities. Ten percent of their income and 10 percent of their leisure time will be donated to civic, charitable, or community causes. Most will be involved in youth baseball, more often as organizers or assistant coaches than YBCs. They lack the competitive drive to be YBCs. You can always pick them out on the sidelines. They are the encouragers, the guys chattering, "Youcandoit-youcandoit-youcandoit."

Second basemen will play baseball until the orthopedic surgeon scrapes away the last of their knee cartilage, then softball—even if they have to switch to first base—until their backs succumb to slipped disks. As their playing days decline, they become ever more vulnerable to the disease of baseballism. They increase their subscriptions to baseball magazines, buy every baseball book on the market, and spend their winters watching Ken Burns's nine-part videotape *Baseball* over and over until they can recite it by heart. Most have such a strong sense of responsibility that they manage to function appropriately, but as children move away and responsibilities diminish, some lose control and become complete fanatics.

As with other obsessions, family members often make excuses for second basemen when they miss work or skip important social functions to sit home and watch games on the tube. In extreme cases, some families have had to forgo health insurance so second basemen could keep their season tickets.

In general, however, baseballism is less problematic than other social disorders since there are normally legal, legitimate, and abundant sources of baseball available; withdrawal seldom occurs. Crises can arise during the off-season, but Thanksgiving and Christmas usually provide sufficient distractions, particularly if the second baseman receives baseball-oriented gifts. The greatest perils are caused by work stoppages and lockouts which disrupt the regular season. The prospect of another World Series cancellation is too horrible to imagine. It simply must not ever occur again. Even in the best of times, life with a baseball fanatic involves sacrifice and accommodation, but most families of second basemen are sympathetic and supportive. After all, the second baseman practically comes with warning labels so no wife can complain she bought a pig in a poke.

When a second baseman reaches his forties or fifties, his wife, children, and friends will chip in to send him to a fantasy spring training camp with retired major leaguers. This will be the best present he ever receives and he will cherish the experience more than his honeymoon. His wife's chagrin will eventually abate when he learns to add (after describing his week in glowing terms), "but I was lonely for my wife the whole time."

In every nursing home in America, from April to October, old men in wheelchairs gather in the lounge to watch baseball on television. Some are blind and can only listen. Many don't remember who they are or know what they are doing. The nurses have wheeled them into the circle for companionship and left them there. Some nod off to sleep and dream, but one or two will be glued to the screen, listening intently to every word of the announcer. They will be wearing brand-new baseball caps, gifts from their grandchildren, and appear to be mumbling to themselves. If you sneak up quietly, you will hear them chanting, "Youcandoit-youcandoit-youcandoit." Don't interrupt them. These men are second basemen and they are making love.

9

The Catcher

First, bless the youthful catchers—in their awkward knee pads and chest pads and masks, their unwieldy tools of ignorance, which shelter all the boys who possess the valor to be catchers.   —*Willie Morris*

The Ingredients

If he were a bird, he'd be a penguin. If he were an amphibian, he'd be a polliwog. If he were a furry critter, he'd be a possum. If he wants to play baseball, he has to be a catcher.

There is no quick test to select an organized youth baseball catcher because YBCs don't need a test. They can spot a catcher from a hundred yards. For one thing, they have no necks. Every one of them looks like the Michelin tire man, one small ball of a head sitting atop one big ball of a body, with arms and legs protruding from the shoulders and butt.

In shape and skill, catchers are the exact opposite of shortstops. Shortstops are lank and lean; catchers are just plain fat. A shortstop's glory is his range; catchers are immobile. Shortstops have quickness, agility, and speed; catchers are sluggish, ungainly, and slow. Shortstops have stamina; catchers take naps between innings, sometimes between pitches. Shortstops have erratic throwing arms; catchers are totally consistent. They can throw it only thirty feet in the air but it goes straight every time.

In fact, catchers and shortstops have but one common trait: both have guts. Catchers are not afraid of the ball. Some say this is because they are stupid, but there are a lot of other stupid people in baseball and most of them at eight years old are petrified of fast-moving spheres. Not catchers.

It's one of the ironies of youth baseball that none of the catcher's physical limitations pose problems. Catchers are perfectly suited and physically appropriate for the demands of their position. They don't have to field and have to throw the ball only about forty feet. Hence, with a ten-foot roll, their thirty feet of hang time is adequate to satisfy their primary throwing responsibility.

This is organized youth baseball at the introductory level, when stealing bases is prohibited so there is no need for a catcher to throw anywhere but to the pitcher. If it's a bunt in the region covered by catchers in higher levels, at the beginning level the catcher cannot reach the ball in time to throw even a fellow catcher out. Hence there is no need, ever, for a catcher to throw the ball to first, second, or third base. Even if the team whips the ball around the bases after a putout, nobody will throw it to the catcher.

Catchers don't have to get a jump on the ball, cover any ground, or run, leap, or dive. They barely have to move. Indeed, it's best if they don't move. If they do, the ball tends to get past them. If they hold their ground, they either catch it or the ball bounces off them. It's much better to have the ball bounce off them where they can just pick it up and throw (or roll) it back to the pitcher.

If it gets by them, they have to stand up (which takes time), walk to the backstop (which takes time), pick up the ball (which takes time), throw it halfway to the pitcher (which takes time), walk up to the ball (which takes time), pick it up again (which takes time), and throw (or roll) it the rest of the way to the pitcher. That's why it's better if catchers don't move. It knocks darn close to an hour off the time it takes to play a game.

Catchers do not cause YBCs any problems. They don't complain about being catchers; they are happy to have a place of their own. Other kids don't want to play the position and catchers don't want to play anywhere but. Anywhere else and they might have to move.

Catchers were always premature at birth and their physical and emotional maturity usually lag behind their age-mates'. Worrisome parents, particularly mother types, have been overfeeding them to compensate for their low birth weights since they came home from the hospital. By the time they arrive at baseball tryouts, their torsos are as plump as a Thanksgiving turkey. However, for reasons that baffle nutritionists, their arms and legs have developed normally. This combination accounts for the catcher's unique Frosty the Snowman physique.

The catcher has come to tryouts at the suggestion of his pediatrician, who thinks exercise would do him some good. Most pediatricians are former second basemen or left fielders. The former so love baseball they will prescribe it as an antidote for any common childhood ailment, and the latter remember little about the sport and have completely forgotten that catchers get about as much exercise as trees.

The catcher comes to tryouts eating an ice cream cone and he has a chocolate bar in his pocket for the break. This is usually stolen by the first baseman. While this is not the first occasion that the catcher has been tormented by a bigger child—it happens frequently in the school yard—he had better expectations of baseball and starts to cry.

Crying at tryouts is not confined to catchers, however, and it would be a gross error to decide all the kids with tears in their eyes are destined to wear the tools of ignorance. If he's crying because someone stole his candy bar, he's a catcher. If he's crying because he doesn't want to be there, he's a right fielder. If he's crying because he can't remember where he is or what he's doing, he's a third baseman. And if he's crying because the shortstop just kicked him in the balls for stealing the fat kid's candy bar, he's a first baseman. Crying at tryouts is too common an occurrence to make an immediate judgment about the weeper's future position in the field or in life.

While a test is unnecessary for selecting catchers, one is offered for the sake of homogeneity. Every other position has one; catchers should too. Get out a stopwatch. Clock the kids sprinting from home plate to first. Now clock them again over the same course but this time tell them to roll the distance. One kid rolled three times faster than he ran. That's the catcher.

The Mold

Because catchers play the entire game in foul territory, they are set apart from their teammates. From the get-go, they are harassed and teased by other players. Right fielders get abused verbally, but the catcher is the butt of all practical jokes. When the first baseman grabs a hat for keep-away, it's always the catcher's. When the pitcher squeezes whipped cream into a glove, it's the catcher's mitt. When the triumvirate—that is, the pitcher–first baseman–center fielder clique—starts squirting somebody with the water bottles, it's always the catcher who looks like he wet his pants. When the catcher, who is emotionally immature, starts to cry, it's always the shortstop who comes to his rescue.

The catcher worships the shortstop. The shortstop represents everything the catcher aspires to be: thin, fast, cocky, bold, brash, and able to put bullies in their places. Still, he worships from afar.

There are too many physical dissimilarities for bonding, but he watches and learns. Catchers and shortstops have common souls; it's the bodies that are different in the extreme. Plus, the catcher has patience, a trait unknown to shortstops.

The catcher's first friend on the team will be the third baseman. Their common bond is dysfunction; both are inept. The third baseman has the physical ability but not the mental capacity; the catcher has the smarts but not the finesse. They sit together at the end of the bench, play catch together and hang out, even though the third baseman never remembers the catcher's name.

The catcher admires the second baseman for his virtue, his seriousness, and his devotion to the game. He looks upon the second baseman as a role model. From his perspective behind the plate, he has a grand view of all the infield action and develops a fairly good understanding of the mechanics of the game as the season progresses.

The catcher dreams of playing either shortstop or second base and many who stick with baseball eventually take up those positions. Likewise, many shortstops switch to catcher in their older years, lured by the opportunity for home plate collisions. Some second basemen also try catching at some time in their long careers but always return to their first love, the keystone sack.

Even though the pitcher and catcher are battery mates, there is no love lost between them. Pitchers dump on catchers. Whenever they throw wild pitches that end up by the backstop or out in the parking lot, they scream at the catcher and blame his—pick one—blindness, clumsiness, or (the worst of all insults) chickening out. Catchers are young, immature, fat, and shy but they are not chicken.

When the pitcher throws high, low, inside, and outside—everywhere but over the plate—and his coach/dad comes to the mound, the first words out of the kid's mouth are, "He's not giving me a target!" Catchers are too bashful for confrontation, particularly with the YBC and his son, but resentment builds, and in baseball as in life there is always a comeuppance and moment of reckoning.

The catcher also resents the first baseman, who is the pitcher's best friend, and the center fielder, who is always sucking up to the YBC through his son. No one on the team develops loves and hates like the catcher. It's his job to count balls and strikes; it's his nature to keep score, and he keeps score on all his teammates.

The catcher's extra gear also sets him apart. He wears his hat backward, covers his face with a mask, his belly with an extra large bib, and his legs with shin guards. Many casual observers think this is what makes catchers walk funny. Untrue. Catchers naturally walk funny because their center of gravity is about fifteen inches east of their spine. The gear is just a convenient excuse for the silly gait.

Catchers also wear a cup. This is a point of pride among catchers but a topic of derision by the triumvirate, who are jealous that their jewels, the center of manhood, are not so highly prized as to merit protection. It's the cup that makes catchers strut, and though they shed the other gear to bat, they retain the cup like Teamsters hold on to their union cards.

Of all the changes that happen to kids in youth baseball, the oddest is what happens to the catcher. He improves. The season is twelve to fifteen games long. Each game is seven innings. An average of six batters come to the plate in every half inning; each batter faces an average of five pitches. In the course of a season, the catcher tries to catch the ball twenty-five hundred to three thousand times.

Since the pitchers occasionally change, no one has the depth and extent of experience trying to catch the ball that the catcher has. That's why we call them catchers.

Eighty percent of the time the catcher tries to catch the ball, he will have to try and throw/roll the ball back to the pitcher. The other 20 percent of the time, the ball is struck, fair or foul, and somebody else gets a chance to have a meaningful relationship with the ball. Again, no one on the team comes close to throwing the ball as often as the catcher.

So catchers improve. By the end of the season, they can throw the ball in the air all the way to the pitcher and catch all but the wildest of pitches thrown. Since organized youth baseball began, every team that bestows an award to the most improved player has given the honor to its catcher. Pitchers receive the MVPs but catchers are truly the MIPs.

Improvement in catching and throwing is like a pebble dropped into the catcher's sense of self. The ripples spread into all aspects of the catcher's life. Catchers lose weight; they become more mobile; they develop hand quickness, then foot quickness, and finally, speed. Their leg muscles become strengthened from squatting and standing three thousand times in the two-month season. Their confidence improves.

The team has a party after the last game and everybody says good-bye until next year. As everybody is slapping hands and backs and butts, the first baseman smacks the catcher in an unfriendly manner, one last poke for the road. The catcher protests and a fight ensues.

It's a short fight. The catcher squats under the bigger kid's reach, tackles him waist-high, sits on his chest, puts his knees on the first baseman's biceps, and makes him say, "I quit." Then, "I'm sorry." Some catchers make the bully go through a litany of "I'm sorries," beginning with "that I took your candy bar."

When the party breaks up and the kids walk off the field, the catcher struts, even without his cup. Walking amid his role models, the shortstop and the second baseman, he is now a man among equals. The only season a catcher is ever bullied and teased is his first. Forever afterward, he's a team leader. That's why the other kids start to wear their caps backward.

The Finished Product

Visit the steam room of your local fitness center or YMCA. Fat, middle-aged men with towels around their waists sit on wooden bleachers sweating like pigs on spits. On the average they are thirty or forty pounds overweight. Just for the heck of it ask if there is someone there named "Chubby." A guy with a build like Bruno Sanmartino stands up—he's got the only athletic build in the room—and says, "That's me." He's a catcher. Don't shake hands with him if you value the integrity of your finger bones.

Once catchers get in shape, they stay in shape all their lives. They do push-ups when they're eighty, oftentimes one-handed. Their stomachs, even if beer-bellied, are hard as rocks. Introductory handshakes with them are contests to determine the better man. Whoever winces loses. They might be husky and brawny, but once they shed that baby fat, they never get fat again.

Nevertheless, nicknames bestowed on them by shortstops in the first year of baseball stick for life. That's why Carlton Fisk is still called Pudge. Any adult who still uses a nickname like Chub, Pudge, Hog, Bull, Tub, Bulldog, or Pig Face was a catcher. Anyone else with such a moniker might consider relocating to drop the tag, but a catcher wears the label with pride.

No matter how tall, slim, trim, or svelte a catcher becomes, he will always be a butterball at his core. He will have the sensitivity and easily hurt feelings of a picked-on kid and he, a natural scorekeeper, will never forget or forgive an unkindness. If you desire your sons to reach old age, teach them the three basic rules of survival: don't sword-fight with Zorro; don't draw on the Two-Gun Kid; and don't make fun of a catcher.

A catcher learns at eight years of age that he can succeed with perseverance and he will always be a stubborn, hardworking, never-say-die man. Whatever path he travels, he will succeed. He will never turn his back on a friend nor his cheek to an enemy. Befriend a catcher and you'll have a friend for life; cross one and you'll never enjoy another good night's sleep.

Catchers are B students at every level. They grind out grades like shortstops grind out Baltimore chops. Likewise in work and romance, the catcher is persistent to the point of being relentless. They have this attitude that all good things come to the tenacious. John Paul Jones of "Don't give up the ship" fame was a catcher.

Many catchers gravitate toward careers in the military, particularly the marines and army infantry. They like the feel of the combat gear. Their favorite part of the war is when the enemy launches a gas attack and they can put on their gas masks.

Catchers have a peculiar trait that polite society finds annoying. No matter how formal the occasion, before standing, sitting, or walking, a catcher will reach down and adjust the clothing around his crotch. This habit is an outgrowth of positioning the cup before moving and is impossible to overcome.

Former catchers are highly recruited by the Mafia to collect overdue payments on installment loans. Remember how the catcher made the first baseman say "I'm sorry"? This is a marketable skill that can be developed into a career. If your favorite athletic teams have demonstrated a frustrating inability to cover the point spread, resulting in cash flow problems, and a visitor to your home or business arrives with his hat on backward and a baseball bat in his hand, you are about to play ball with a former catcher. This is not a fun game. If you have no other assets readily convertible to cash, your firstborn child will soon begin a dancing career in a glass booth on Times Square.

The best detectives and FBI agents are all former catchers. J. Edgar Hoover was a classic backstop who exhibited all the telltale signs. The man, like a bulldog, had no discernible neck and jowls. He loved wearing bulletproof vests, believed in physical training, kept score on everybody in America, relentlessly pursued wise guys, and was fond of touching his scrotum even while talking to presidents.

Catchers enter the legal profession in numbers far greater than their proportion in the population and most often choose trial work. If you are accused of a crime and the prosecutor scratches his nuts before beginning his opening remarks to the jury, you're in big trouble. You will save yourself time and anxiety by switching your plea to guilty and accepting life imprisonment—unless your own lawyer, after being introduced to you, extends his hand and says, "My friends call me Chub." If that's the case, sit back and enjoy the spectacle. The trial will be so entertaining, you'll forget it's your own life at stake in the outcome.

As fathers, catchers make hard taskmasters. They live disciplined lives and demand much of their children. They believe in rules; they demand obedience. If your father is fond of quoting the Fourth Commandment (Honor thy father), he was probably a catcher. Some become control freaks and try to dictate their children's life choices. If your father summons you to the living room and introduces you to the offspring of his best friend with the words, "This is the person I want you to marry," you were sired by a catcher. Chances are he calls your mother his "battery mate."

A word of caution. Be faithful to your spouse if your father-in-law was a catcher, particularly if he is a trial lawyer or does odd jobs for a guy whose last name ends with a vowel.

Catchers, more than anyone else, see themselves in terms of their position. A man may become a judge, the head of the FBI, the captain of a ship or an industry, or the don of a family whose members kiss each other on the cheek, but if he strapped on shin guards and a chest protector when he was eight years old and you ask him what he is, he'll automatically respond, "A catcher."

Some take the position with them to the grave. It is relatively rare but not unheard of for a backstopper to have CATCHER chiseled on his headstone.

If you meet one for the first time and converse for more than six minutes, he will somehow squeeze into the conversation that he used to be a catcher. This is unnecessary; you already knew it. When he stood up to greet you, he scratched his balls. When he shook your hand, he broke two of your favorite fingers. When his name was revealed, he added proudly, "But my friends call me Tubby."

10

The Center Fielder

Just to have his body, I'd trade mine and my wife's and throw in some
cash.
                                        —*Pete Rose on Mike Schmidt*

Ingredients

In the beginning of the year, the league will issue each YBC six
baseballs that are expected to last the season. After every practice, one will be missing. The YBC calls the kids in and tells them
nobody can go home until the lost ball is located. One player
looks around quickly and, whether it's in the tall weeds at the
base of the backstop or nestled in the outfield dandelions, he
hollers, "There it is," and runs to fetch it. He covers the distance
in long, graceful strides, scoops up the ball, and pegs it in. No
matter how far away he is, the ball stings the YBC's palm. That
kid is the center fielder.

Put all nine players in a clump somewhere in the outfield, stay
at home plate and hit a half dozen fungoes toward the middle of

the group. The same kid will catch them all. After each catch, he'll fire a return throw that will skim the pitcher's mound and bounce to your chest. Call him in to catch for you while you're hitting.

Hit a half dozen more to the group. Three or four different players will call for them; half will be caught, half will be bobbled. None of the return throws, even the pitcher's, will quite make second base. The kid standing at your elbow is the center fielder.

He's splinter thin, tall, and fluid. He moves like he doesn't have a bone in his body. Some kids can catch, some can throw; but only the center fielder can do both naturally. Everything looks like it comes easy for him. It does. It's not the arm or the glove, the arm-glove combination, or the coordination that distinguishes center fielders. It's the eyes. Center fielders see so well, it appears that they know where the ball is going before the ball is struck. Some call it depth perception; some think it's ESP.

The center fielder is the fastest runner on the team, but he looks slow. In a footrace the shortstop will take three strides for every one of the center fielder's and beat him by a step at the wire, but that's just shortstop pride. On a stopwatch, nobody turns in better times than the center fielder.

Center fielders do not misjudge fly balls. Most kids run on their heels, which jars the spine and blurs the vision, causing them to lose the ball. Not center fielders. They run on the balls of their feet. It's total toe-to-eye coordination. Without instruction or experience, they naturally catch line drives shoulder high, to be in immediate throwing position; charge ground balls; and always throw in front of the runner.

The center fielder never mentions his father, and his father never comes to a practice or a game. His father may be divorced and live in another community or he may be a workaholic, an airline pilot, or a long distance trucker. The kid might not even have a dad. There's an aura of space around the center fielder, a sense of distance in all his relationships. Though he chums with the pitcher and first baseman, he never tries to get close to anyone except the YBC, whom he idolizes and shadows like a puppy.

The center fielder sits beside the YBC in the dugout, helps him load the gear in the trunk after practices, and after a few weeks of getting himself noticed and recognized, persistently hints for a ride home. He calls the YBC "Coach" and breathes the word like it was the beginning of a prayer.

His mother is nearly as invisible as his father. When she drops him off just in sight of the field, she stays in her car, but even at a distance the coaches and parents—particularly the fathers—notice her long legs, bare midriff, and peroxided hair. She's a beautiful woman in a hurry, pleased that her son will be occupied for several hours. There's a karma of mystery to her that even the center fielder does not understand.

His first friend on the team is the second baseman. The center fielder's mother is always late to pick him up and the second baseman will hang around the field playing catch with him until she arrives. The second baseman will never leave if there's someone—anyone—left to keep playing ball. If there are no humans available, he'll play fetch with a dog until the mutt quits.

Eventually, the center fielder seeks out the pitcher, who's the YBC's son, as his best friend. He does this by blowing smoke. He appeals to the pitcher's vanity, praising his fastball, knocking umps who called too many balls, pointing out the pitcher's poise on the mound and his power at the plate. The pitcher sucks it all in. The center fielder also ingratiates himself to the YBC by praising his son. He maneuvers invitations to the pitcher's house after school and on weekends; once there, he focuses his attention and conversation on the YBC. Once camaraderie with the pitcher is forged, the second baseman's friendship is dropped like a screamer to the hot corner.

By the end of the season the pitcher, first baseman, and center fielder will be a triumvirate; the second baseman and shortstop will be lifelong buddies; and the third baseman and catcher, the team's odd couple. The left fielder will be content in his own company, and the right fielder will be a stranger in everybody's world, including his own.

The center of the triumvirate will be the pitcher, the first baseman will always feel second best, and the center fielder will be the odd man out in every dispute. All outfielders will be somewhat isolated; the left fielder by his choice, the right fielder by everyone else's choice, and the center fielder by nature. The center fielder will swallow a lot of pride to be included in the triumvirate, but the trade-off—humiliation by the YBC's son in exchange for time, attention, and affection from the YBC—will be worth it to him.

The Mold

In truth, the center fielder is the outfield. The right fielder is useless; the left fielder, clueless. The center fielder takes off at the crack of the bat to be wherever the ball is going. He tries to back up the entire infield and does an adequate job unless the ball is tight to either of the foul lines. Then he must scream at his outfield mates to fetch the ball and throw it to him for the relay in. The YBC's instructions to him are to call for every ball he can possibly reach, and the left fielder and right fielder are told to defer to him in all matters of judgment.

The center fielder takes his responsibilities seriously and acquires an anxious personality because of his overwhelming burden. Many develop tics and nervous twitches. Paranoia is not uncommon. To fail to reach a ball in time to limit the base runner to a double is to fail the YBC, to disappoint him. To avoid this catastrophe, the center fielder will give his all. His sleep before games will be filled with nightmares of fly balls that hug the lines and drop fair. Center fielders wake up wet with sweat and frequently fall out of bed lunging for balls in their sleep.

Center fielders grow to loathe right fielders and left fielders and later in life exhibit apathy toward the handicapped and antipathy toward intellectuals, free spirits, and liberals.

Fortunately for center fielders, few youth baseball players can get around on the ball enough to pull it down the left field line, and balls close to the right foul line slice as they lose their oomph. Most of the ground balls hit into the outfield will be gappers and the center fielder with his good eyes and his quick start will be able to hold even the fastest runners to a double.

Center fielders are crowd thrillers and YBC pleasers. Only once a game will they catch a line drive or fly ball, but it will always kill the other team's rally and be the most exciting and memorable defensive play of the game. The catch is always for the third out, and the center fielder receives instant gratification from the YBC as he hustles to the dugout with his glove hand in the air with the ball protruding from the top of the webbing like a scoop of vanilla on an ice cream cone.

For some unexplained reason, the center fielder always leads off the next inning with a solo home run. This perplexing occurrence happens at every level of baseball, including the major leagues.

Twice in a typical twelve-game season, a big-bellied, skinny-legged catcher will swat a hard grounder up the middle and start chugging toward first. The center fielder will charge the ball recklessly, scoop it barehanded, and gun a perfect throw to the first baseman for the force out at first.

These two plays will forever be featured in the center fielder's lifetime highlights film, and he will never forget the names or faces of the catchers so that whenever he meets one at life's invariable intersections, he can say, "Remember me? I'm the center fielder who threw you out at first." The catcher will study him for a few moments, searching his memory for recognition, and finally ask, "Oh yeah, which one?"

The Finished Product

The center fielder's lifetime legacy from his first year of baseball will be anxiety. Not as inherently dangerous as the first baseman's anger, it still infects the center fielder's mind like anger taxes the first baseman's heart. He will be suspicious of all love offered him and always feel that another's affection is contingent on his successful performance in the field.

He will need constant validation. He will require a good job at a good salary, prestige in the community, and material evidence of success in order to feel secure.

Fortunately for the center fielder, these accomplishments and symbols will come his way—because of his sense of responsibility and his determination to have them. He will drive a late-model, expensive car and wear a suit and tie to whatever job he holds. He will be reserved and aloof to co-workers, obsequious to supervisors, and remote to family members.

He will never lose the aura of space about him, and even his wife and children will feel distant from him. He will give them everything money can buy but little of himself. They will have a sense of something missing but never be able to identify exactly what it is or to persuade him to discuss it with them. He will never admit it, but he'll know.

Golf or pool will be his main post-baseball athletic activity. If he chooses the links, his handicap will be in the single digits. Even after he retires, he will win his club championship and scads of tournaments. His equipment will be the finest and most expensive, but he will never ride a cart. He may use a caddy or rent a cart for his partner and clubs but he will always walk by himself.

He will be a superb putter and have a collection of old wooden blades displayed in his recreation room. In every round he ever plays, he will hit at least one spectacular shot that will be the talk of the clubhouse for the evening. In his career, he will have multiple holes-in-one and at least one double eagle. Questioned about his uncanny luck, he'll wink with one eye and point to the other. "The eyes have it" will be his only reply.

If the center fielder chooses pool, he will never have to buy a beer in a bar with a table. No one will beat him and he will regularly run the table before his opponent gets a shot. Knocking the eight ball in on the break will not be an uncommon occurrence. Bank shots will be his specialty but he will also be adept at massé shots and cue ball positioning. He will have a half dozen fail-safe trick shots good for winning small wagers and entertaining bystanders. People will always enjoy watching him but few will ever invite him over to sit and chew the fat.

Politically, a center fielder will have no set agenda but will choose his positions from the negative, always being anti-something, never in favor of an alternative. He will despise liberals, special interest groups, the income tax, social causes, and minority rights, but keep his distance from right wing groups as well. He will never be a joiner, never vote in a primary, and always register as an independent.

Socially, he will be good company and a solid—but never intimate—friend. His associates will regard him highly and seek his business advice but never his emotional support. In his career, the center fielder will seek a mentor, an older man he admires and respects to the edge of worship. This mentor will be a man of authority who can and will facilitate the center fielder's professional advancement. The older man will proudly claim the younger as his protégé but the younger will be insecure and constantly seek reassurances from the older.

Romantically, the center fielder will be chivalrous, courtly, and slightly aggressive. He will be attracted to only the most comely women and dote on them until he captures their fancy. Afterward, he will move on to newer challenges. He will exhibit his woman like an expensive car or a graphite driver.

Eventually, the center fielder will encounter a woman who remains impervious to his charm and costly gifts. When he cannot overcome her nonchalance and indifference, he will propose, she will accept, and he will be hers as long as she does not become totally his. If the point comes when she desires him more than, or even as much as, he desires her, the contest will be over and he will have won. He will then find a younger, more attractive and elusive woman to be his mistress or mate.

Emotionally, the center fielder will always be the can-do kid who snagged the line drive with an over-the-shoulder catch and who hit the grand slam home run to win the game in the last inning. All his life he will be able to bring the crowd to its feet celebrating and cheering his accomplishments.

And the crowd always will be a throng of strangers, his father will be far away, and his mother will be off doing errands. When the bleachers empty and the crowd disperses, he'll be who he was at eight years old: a little boy alone, waiting for his ride home.

11

The Third Baseman

I'll tell you how smart Pete is. When they had a blackout in New York, he was stranded thirteen hours on an escalator.

—*Joe Nuxhall on third baseman Pete Rose*

Ingredients

At some point early in the season, a batter will catch just a piece of the ball, yielding a slow grounder. A fielder will charge in, scoop the ball with his bare hand, throw with all his power, and drill the batter in the small of the back. "Gotcha! Yer out," he'll holler with pride. After the medics cart off the wounded batter, the YBC will try to explain to his fielder that that particular rule of baseball was eliminated around 1849.

Shortly afterward, a cleanup batter will get around on the ball and send a screaming line drive toward the same player, who will dive to the dirt, successfully avoiding the baseball, and then jump up singing, "Nah-nah, ya missed me, now ya gotta kiss me."

That's the third baseman. He confuses baseball with dodgeball and never quite figures out the differences. He's a good kid but dumber than dirt. There's an acid test for third basemen, works every time. Ask him to spell *ox* and give him the first two letters. This poser has stumped third basemen for generations.

Third basemen are difficult to coach because they take everything literally, and baseball is a game of poetic imagery. The third baseman knows he's no rocket scientist so he concentrates fully and obeys absolutely. Suppose his team is at bat with two outs and, by some miracle, he makes it to second base. The YBC yells to him, "As soon as the ball is hit, take third and run home."

If the next batter hits the ball, the third baseman will run to third base, dig the bag up with his heels, and take it to his house as fast as he can. If you see a youth baseball game and they're using a Frisbee for third, you can bet the farm that some YBC told his third baseman to "take third and run home."

The main reason a kid is put at third is because the base is next to the visitors' dugout. Third basemen get first and third mixed up, particularly on unfamiliar diamonds, and it's easier to walk the kid to his position if it's close by. This also allows the YBC to maintain vocal contact with the third baseman in case the kid forgets where he is or what he is doing there. Generally speaking, rotations confuse third basemen and they don't know enough to come back to the dugout after the third out. The closer he is, the easier it is to send someone to escort him back to the bench. At home games, there's always a parent who will volunteer to sit on the visitors' side to provide these services.

If the "spell ox" test doesn't work because several of the kids on the team are stymied by it, there's one other sure method to identify who should play the hot corner. The third baseman's parents call him "Sonny." If he has an older brother, his sibling's name is "Big Sonny." If he also has a little brother, the youngest is called "Little Sonny," and he becomes "Middle Sonny." If a fourth son is born, that child is given up for adoption.

If you ask the third baseman's father his son's real name, the father will need to check with the mother and she will answer, "I don't know but I'll check in the Bible." These initial three words—"I don't know"—account for two thirds of the words a YBC will hear from the kid on the hot corner in the course of the season. In fact, that percentage will hold true for the entire family. That's why Bud Abbott, in his famous comedy routine with Lou Costello, named his third baseman "I Don't Know."

Incidentally, if the third baseman has a sister, he calls her "Sis." If he has two, they are "Big Sis" and "Little Sis." Don't bother asking him their given names because you know what his answer will be. Don't ask his mother either unless she's toting the family Bible.

Besides being dumb, the third baseman is dirty. The character Pig-Pen in the *Peanuts* cartoons is a typical third baseman. No third baseman ever washes his uniform, and by the end of the season it's a different color than all of his teammates'. No matter how grimy and grubby he is at the start of the game, he's dirtier at the end, even if he had no chances in the field and struck out every at bat. Third basemen attract grime like belly buttons attract lint. They blend in so well with the base path that sometimes the only way to spot a third baseman is if he moves. YBCs yell to the infielders to move up on the infield grass when a batter shows bunt or when he wants to find his third baseman.

Third basemen are mules. They have little talent but they try like hell to learn how to play. As primitives, their instincts are to avoid fast-moving balls, and it takes sheer force of will for them not to duck line drives or jump away from hard grounders. Still, by the end of the season, they will block all but the hardest hit balls with their bodies.

They can't catch or throw, of course, but that doesn't matter. The YBC knows that in the entire season of fifteen games his team will effect 315 outs and the third baseman will be involved in only four or five of them. About once every three games there will be men on first and second and a ball will be drilled to the hot corner. The third baseman will knock it down with his body, pick it up, and tag his base before the runner arrives. This will account for a third of the team's seasonal total of fifteen mystery outs.

Normally, all a YBC wants from his third baseman is to keep the ball in the infield to prevent extra bases. This he will do. In fact, a third baseman will do anything and everything a YBC requests as long as it does not require talent or thought.

The Mold

A third baseman in organized youth baseball has never affected the outcome of a game. If he scores a run, his team will win by two or more. If his fielding stops a run from scoring, his team will win or lose by at least four. If his baserunning causes his team to lose a sure scoring opportunity—third basemen have a tendency to run the wrong way after getting on base—it will not affect the game's outcome. Nor will his errors. Not enough playable balls are hit in his direction. Almost anything he can get to, the shortstop will get to first. He is as useless as three extra strikes are to a right fielder.

Being stupid, he is blissfully unaware of this lack of utility and will gradually improve in all aspects of the game. He likes baseball. He likes the coach. He likes being part of a team. He is good-natured enough to be unoffended by the razzing he takes from the pitcher, center fielder, and first baseman, and if one of them ever does hurt his feelings, he likes the way the shortstop rises to his defense.

The third baseman becomes chums with the catcher, even though he never remembers his name. He befriends and defends the right fielder the way the shortstop stands up for him. For the first and perhaps only time in his life, he has someone to whom he is naturally superior.

During the season, he learns to adjust. He can never remember if it's three strikes and four balls or four strikes and three balls, but learns that if he just gets back in the batter's box after every pitch, sooner or later the umpire will point to either first base or his dugout. Occasionally he gets confused and when the ump points to the dugout, he goes and stands on third base, but the frequency of this error diminishes as the season progresses.

He does not like the YBC yelling at him, particularly when he does what the YBC says and gets in trouble. Like the time the YBC told him to hold the runner on third base and then hollered at him for grabbing the kid's belt. It was the other team's first baseman, who was very big, but he did his best and hung on tight even after being dragged to the plate. Another time he got blasted for tackling the kid rounding third when the YBC yelled at him to stop the runner. Despite all the shouting, he was proud that he did his job.

Early on, the third baseman occasionally puts his glove on the wrong hand but figures out that hitting himself in the ear while throwing the ball is a signal to switch the glove to the other hand. This discovery is his own and will be the source of great pride, particularly when he passes the information on to Big Sonny and it works for him, too. In return for that tip, his brother discloses a secret for figuring out which hand goes on top when gripping the bat to hit.

"Anytime you swing at the ball and hit the catcher in the head, you should switch hands," Big Sonny tells him. Thus begins a lifelong brotherly bond with Big Sonny, and the third baseman owes it all to baseball, which is the third reason why he likes the game so much.

The Finished Product

Third basemen stick with baseball through thick and thin. While they might try other sports, baseball always remains their favorite. This is due to their enhanced sense of accomplishment in learning such things as finding their own base, which hand to put the glove on, and the proper position of the hands when batting. They never try any position other than third, that being difficult enough to master in one lifetime, and through time, sweat, and effort become quite accomplished. They learn to sacrifice their bodies and to play hurt. People come to call them "gutsy" and "gritty" and "aggressive."

A pattern develops. Third basemen try something new and fail miserably but don't quit. They stick to it. Eventually, if the task requires neither talent nor thought, they master it. The world acknowledges their success; they feel good about themselves and keep doing the same thing over and over until they become one with the task. Frequently, fourth grade is like that. The third baseman is baffled by geography, spelling, history, and counting. He flunks but stays with it, returning until he can name the seven continents, spell "Sonny," and count to one hundred with his eyes closed.

The first job a third baseman lands when he quits school at sixteen will become his career. He will work that same job until age sixty-five without taking a single sick day and never be bored. Third basemen like jobs that require uniforms and getting dirty. They become garage mechanics, soldiers, plumbers, steamfitters, ironworkers, and Maytag repairmen. They don't mind working in heat, rain, or snow and often supplement their incomes with second jobs.

Third basemen are not wasteful, flashy, or flamboyant. They save their money and buy what they buy, including cars and houses, with cash. By age fifty, they usually have enough put away for a little spread in Florida and enough seniority on the job—they've been at the same one for thirty-four years—to take the whole month of February off and spend it in the sun with the old lady.

Third basemen like loud machines. They go to tractor pulls and stock car races. If they don't farm a few acres for the hell of it, they have friends who do, and they spend their days off driving farm machines through the fields, planting, cultivating, spraying, and harvesting. They buy snowmobiles and all-terrain vehicles. Their snowblowers and lawn mowers are louder than the Concorde, and they are likely to have a tractor, bulldozer, or backhoe in the garage for odd jobs.

Their vehicle of choice is a pickup truck and they stock it with gun racks and toolboxes. Often they have two trucks: one for working, the other for formal occasions, such as weddings, retirement parties, and bowling banquets. A third baseman always has grease under his fingernails, mud on his boots, and grime ground into his work clothes. On the other hand, the cab of his special-occasion pickup, his workshop floor, and his garage are clean enough to eat off.

Third basemen start dating late but their courtships are short and they marry young, certainly by age twenty-three. Their wives must learn to tolerate their long work hours and their beering with the boys on weekends, and unless the wife wants trouble she'd better have the house clean, the laundry done, and hot victuals on the table when her third baseman pulls into the driveway.

Third basemen stay married as long as the wife obeys his three simple rules, whatever they are. If their marriages do go bust, they do not remain single but marry some other third baseman's ex-wife within three years. It's an old third baseman's trick to always get married on the anniversary of his first marriage so that he will not have to remember another date.

Third basemen are men of habit. They get up at the same time every morning, usually about 5 A.M., eat lunch at the same diner every day, and stop at the same joint on the way home every night. They read the same paper at the same time every day, bowl with the same team on Thursday nights every summer, and play cards with Big Sonny in the same league every winter. Every Sunday night at 10 P.M., the third baseman makes love to his wife even if there's been a fight and he's not talking to her.

Third basemen never get smart but grow wise with age. They never forget a face or remember a name. They learn three little rules that apply to all of life's situations, which they employ over and over again. Once they master a skill, they never forget it. They make a lot of mistakes in their lives, but never the same one more than three times.

Third basemen are not philosophers but they wonder why threes keep popping up in their lives. Each third baseman has three jokes, three stories, and three memories that he repeats when the occasion calls for it; one of each is about baseball. He also has three friends he cherishes, three women he loves, three wishes for his children, and three secrets, one that he shares with his wife, one that he shares with Big Sonny, and one that he keeps all to himself.

12

The Left Fielder

Do you realize that even as we sit here, we are hurtling through space at a tremendous rate of speed? Think about it. Our world is just a hanging curve ball.
                                                                            —*Bill Lee*

Nothing can bring back the hour
Of splendor in the grass
Of glory in the flower . . .   —*William Wordsworth*

Ingredients

Here's a paradox impossible to explain. Baseball fans are the most intelligent, articulate, and thoughtful of all followers of American sports. "The Game" appeals to scientists, mathematicians, poets, writers, CEOs, philosophers, and librarians, people who earn their daily bread pondering, contemplating, and reflecting on the mysteries of the universe. The intelligentsia. The brains of the country. The players and managers, on the other hand, are, to be charitable, morons. Then again, why be charitable?

Participants in the game of baseball, from owners to peanut vendors, are the dumbest creatures allowed to roam at large in a free society. Any journalist who has ever tried to do a postgame interview of a baseball player knows this. With ten tries, not one in ten can construct a sentence that contains both a noun and a verb—the reference being to the player, not the journalist. That's why the few with triple-figure wattage, like Reggie Jackson and Bill Lee, become such bright lights and receive all the media attention.

Dizzy Dean quit school in second grade and when asked about it confessed, "I didn't do so great in first grade, either." Still, he felt blessed because "the good Lord was good to me. He gave me a strong body, a good right arm, and a weak mind." These, he felt, were the three essentials of a baseball player, and who would know better than Dizzy Dean?

There is nothing as rare in baseball as a player whose cranium contains less cork than Albert Belle's bat. Players are issued spikes to keep their feet embedded in the soil. Otherwise, these light heads would float into the stands with every stiff breeze to center field.

There's an explanation for this phenomenon. Baseball is all stop and go, inaction and action, wait and hurry. Thoughts are a distraction during the pauses and worthless during the action, which occurs so quickly that responses must be instinctive. If one stops to think what to do, it's too late to do it. Thinkers are weeded out of baseball over time so that only the blank screens make it to The Show.

Most eight-year-olds are too mentally immature and undeveloped for thoughts, so thinking normally does not interfere with performance at the entry level. In those rare instances in organized youth baseball when a YBC gets stuck with a kid with ample gray matter to have thoughts, there is only one thing to do with him. Put him in left field.

Left fielders love baseball almost as much as second basemen but for different reasons. Second basemen love the action; left fielders love the inaction. Second basemen love to field balls; left fielders view balls hit to them as unwanted intrusions into their quiet time. Second basemen focus entirely on the elements of the game: on the batter, the base runners, the positions of their team-mates, the signals from the YBC, and the ball, even when it's in the pitcher's glove; left fielders allow their minds to float free in the outfield. They have thoughts. They watch birds flying over-head and often turn their backs to the infield to see where the birds are going. They stare at the grass, meditate on dandelions, search the area around their feet for four-leaf clovers, and some-times drop to all fours for a closer inspection.

Both second basemen and left fielders cherish extra-inning games; the second basemen because the game goes on, the left fielder because he may get to see the sun set behind the distant hills.

There are telltale signs of a natural left fielder that mark a kid even before the tryouts begin. He arrives with his father, who is carrying a book. As the kids assemble around the YBCs, the fa-ther sits cross-legged in the sun and begins to read, oblivious to the efforts of his child on the field.

When the wannabes begin the fielding portion of the tryout, the left fielder asks the YBCs if there's an extra glove around; he forgot his. When the left fielder steps to the plate for the hitting portion of the tryout, he has his hands in reversed position on the bat. When the YBC points out his mistake, he comments, "Per-haps. Conversely, I may have assumed my stance on the improper side of the plate," and without switching hands, he walks around home plate and tries batting from the opposite side. Any other player could not have realized this possibility without an electri-cal current surging between his ears, i.e., he had a thought, there-fore he's a left fielder.

Of all the kids on the team, the left fielder will be the most knowledgeable of the rules and history of baseball. When asked how this is so, he will admit that while trying to decide whether or not to play, he consulted the *Encyclopaedia Britannica*, which he accessed in the Library of Congress through the In-ternet on his personal computer.

He may make unfavorable comparisons of baseball to cricket; he may insist on gripping the bat with his hands six inches apart as Ty Cobb did, and he will cite the Tiger Great's lifetime batting average and major league career records as proof of the superiority of his hand position.

Left fielders show surprising natural ability throwing, hitting, and fielding. Their common denominator, besides intelligence, is potential. YBCs select them early in the draft because they see the innate talent and assume that with proper coaching they can be transformed into ballplayers. This is a mistake. Left fielders are extraterrestrial beings; communication with them is beyond human capability. In all the years of organized youth baseball, only one player who started in left field made it to the majors and that was Bill Lee.

A hundred years of baseball experience and observation is the basis of the expression "out in left field" to describe someone lost in their own world. Before the first season is complete, the wisdom of the saying will be demonstrated anew to every YBC who thought his left fielder a diamond in the rough.

The Mold

Left field is the perfect position for the left fielder. He is situated in the one location on the field where he can dream without diminishing his team's defensive capability. In the entire season, he will not have a single fly ball hit directly to him. No eight-year-old can combine enough power and bat speed to pull a liner to left.

The left fielder's sole responsibility will be to back up the third baseman two or three times a game. For this task he will have the assistance of the center fielder who will, at the precise moment the ball is struck, scream at him to wake up, allowing him adequate time to make an adequate play on the ball. Left fielders do not aspire to surpass adequacy.

The one skill the left fielder will need to develop is keeping open the frequency to his consciousness on which the center fielder chooses to transmit his emergency alert. After a few miscues, the left fielder will respond to the center fielder's cry of "Heads up, asshole, it's your ball," the way combat vets respond to the warning, "Incoming!" He'll stir from his meditations, charge the ball, and flip it in to the shortstop or second baseman, then return to his position and drift back to sleep.

On sunny days, when the bottom of the other team's order comes to bat, it is common for the left fielder to lie down on his back, using his glove for a pillow, and stare at the clouds. YBCs hate this. The left fielder will try to explain logically that it is scientifically impossible for someone in the bottom of the order to hit a ball in his direction and that cloud study is a constructive use of otherwise wasted time.

The logic is irrefutable but the YBC will insist such behavior looks bad. Left fielders, notoriously uninterested in appearances, will boldly defy the YBC's edict against reclining in the field, and simply mumble, "I forgot," when chastised for repeating the forbidden conduct.

Dandelion picking is another occupational habit of left fielders. Like eating peanuts, the behavior is compulsive and impossible to curb once begun. The plucked dandelions end up protruding from those little air holes in the left fielder's baseball cap, then his buttonholes and shoelace holes.

What rankles the YBC most is that the left fielder is able to convince the right fielder, the third baseman, and the catcher that a dandelion is a powerful talisman that will protect them from beanballs, errors, and jammed fingers. All baseball players are superstitious and the lower orders of ballplayers are the most superstitious of all.

The left fielder capitalizes on this foible, and soon half the team look like soldiers in camouflage. Eventually, the YBC explodes and intimidates all but the left fielder into abandoning the custom. The extra dandelions are then given to parents and fans who graciously thank the left fielder, roll their eyes, and—except for his immediate family—innocuously discard the vegetation.

You can always pick out the left fielder's father. He's the guy off to the side, reading a book, with dandelions tucked behind his ears. His mother, in her few appearances, is off in the weeds, dancing barefoot in the sun, twirling her long skirts to reveal her unshaven thighs, and tossing dandelions and buttercups into the breezes.

Because the ball so seldom appears in left field, what occurs there often escapes the attention of the YBC, who, like the second baseman, concentrates on the site of the ball. At least once a game, a left fielder forgets to return to the dugout after the other team's third out.

The new left fielder will see nothing odd about the other's presence and will respect his privacy sufficiently not to disturb the stranger's contemplations; soon he will be lost in his own. It is only when the left fielder's turn at bat arrives and he cannot be found that anyone will think to call out for his return.

No left fielder has ever been embarrassed by this event despite the headshaking and chuckles from the grandstand. He's accustomed to being misunderstood and un-understood. It goes with the territory.

Left fielders, like third basemen, never know the score. It means nothing to them and has no impact on their dispositions. The concept of winning and losing is foreign to their metabolism. Ask a left fielder how the game went and his response will include the number of ladybugs and grasshoppers observed, a report on a titanic struggle between a robin and a worm, and a description of ants carrying a dead fly back to their hill. He'll display his collection of dandelions and buttercups and ask if you want him to gather greens for a salad. He might even offer you a copy of his dad's recipe, but he will never mention an incident or event from the game.

Oblivious as left fielders appear to be about the game itself, they automatically observe, record, and store minutiae about their teammates' performances. If the first baseman grumbles that he should be the leadoff hitter because he has a better batting average than the shortstop, the left fielder is likely to interject,

> Batting average is a negligible factor in determining contributions to run totals. On-base percentage is the only reliable measurement. You're batting .337 but your on-base percentage is only .450; the shortstop bats only .221, but his smaller strike zone produces more walks and his superior footspeed lets him beat the throw on fielders' errors so his on-base percentage is .785. Hence he clearly contributes more significantly to total runs than you do.

This settles the argument and silences the grumbler, though the figures cited are products of imagination rather than memory. Only the second baseman will have an inkling of the fabrication. The left fielder speaks with too much authority to be challenged by his moronic associates. No one can argue with him, not even the YBC.

He uses this talent sparingly and only in defense of the downtrodden. The triumvirate of pitcher, first baseman, and center fielder, the big-boned bullies, quickly learn to hate his guts, while the others, the frequent targets of abuse, rank him alongside the shortstop as a defender of the oppressed. The shortstop does it with his fists and the left fielder with his mouth, but both are proficient at putting the big guys down.

The Finished Product

The most difficult task of this entire project was locating former left fielders to ascertain the lasting effects of playing the position in youth baseball. No one remembered being a left fielder. Ultimately, a backdoor method of identification was devised. Adults who played other positions were asked to identify the left fielders on their teams and those individuals were contacted and asked to complete the questionnaire.

The results were informative. Every single one completed the line "Position Played" with "unknown" or "don't remember." The original questionnaires were then reexamined and the teammates of those who answered the question "unknown" or "don't remember" were contacted with nearly parallel results: 90 percent were left fielders.

The other 10 percent, after stringent cross-examinations and promises of confidentiality, tearfully admitted to being right fielders.

The uniformity among former left fielders was staggering. None were blue-collar workers, none were in private business, and none wore suits and ties to their jobs. In fact, only 8 percent owned suits or ties, and in every instance the outfit was purchased and donned only for a parent's funeral or their own wedding.

Left fielders were predominant in college lecture halls, industrial laboratories, and the medical profession. There were no psychologists or chiropractors but numerous psychiatrists, surgeons, and pediatricians. Sixty-nine percent of the pediatricians had spent at least one year volunteering at an inner-city clinic or in a third-world country.

All botanists were not former baseball players but all botanists who played baseball were left fielders. There were similar findings among college mathematics teachers, archaeologists, astronomers, poets, and philosophers.

Every left fielder who graduated from high school had at least one advanced degree. Next to third basemen and catchers, however, left fielders were the least likely to finish high school. Most gave their reason for quitting as "knew enough," and 70 percent of the left field dropouts obtained GEDs and attended college anyway. Go figure.

All left fielders are leftist in their political persuasion, an amazing number being openly Marxist. Few abused alcohol but many sang the praises of marijuana and some admitted to occasional use. The overwhelming alcoholic beverage of choice was wine. Many had wine cellars and claimed to be connoisseurs, and several were amateur winemakers, dandelion wine being the most popular variety.

The average number of years in baseball was two. None could be found who continued to participate past junior high, but an extremely high proportion maintained their interest as spectators and fans, with the Chicago Cubs and the Boston Red Sox being the clear favorites. This interest in baseball was pure and did not involve wagering on the outcome of games; not betting on games is a phenomenon unique to left fielders and second basemen.

To the query about what aspect of baseball held greatest appeal, all left fielders mentioned ambiance: pretzels and peanuts, the roar of the crowd, the sparkle and smell of freshly mowed outfield grass, the warmth of ballpark sunshine. None mentioned home runs, no-hitters, double plays, stolen bases, or any other of the game's components, the parts chosen by second basemen. Their only shared appreciation was for pretzels and peanuts. Incidentally, both also agreed that baseball was an outdoor activity and reproached playing it under domes.

Although their participation in organized athletics was small, former left fielders remained physically active well into their golden years as skiers, surfers, scullers, mountain climbers, long distance runners, and walkers. Posture was a peculiar point of pride among left fielders, who also frequently noted their height and arm length as natural gifts.

Those who tried other team sports most often listed wide receiver in football and small forward in basketball as their positions and sports. Experience in individual sports happened more often, with track and field being the huge favorite and wrestling, fencing, and handball clumped at a distant second. Though not included in the survey, many mentioned chess as a competitive sport.

Alternative lifestyles were common among former left fielders. If they married at all, they married late in life, the average age being thirty-four. Few were divorced but spouse abandonment and multiple mating were common. Letters were more routinely used for communication with adult children than telephones, and a significant portion had their only phone connected to a fax machine.

Pianos, computers, telescopes, and tropical fish aquariums were more common in their homes than televisions. Seventy-three percent played a musical instrument, clarinets, French horns, and trumpets being the most popular, though a notable number played several instruments. Jazz and blues were their favorite types of music.

Left fielders as a rule are happy with their lot in life and value solitude over friendship and independence over involvement. Many listed their dog as their best friend. They have as few intimates as center fielders and right fielders but unlike the others, this is not a source of distress nor caused by social incompetence. It is a preference and a matter of choice.

Whatever the area of a left fielder's life—occupation, education, athletics, or intimate relationships—in the judgment of others, he will fail to live up to his potential. This causes the left fielder no anxiety as he has no motive, inclination, or drive to fulfill anyone's expectations but his own. He emerged from his baseball experience impervious to public pressure, undeterred by public censure, and unswayed by public flattery.

Our survey merely scratched the surface of defining, pigeon-holing, and understanding former left fielders. In fact, they resisted the whole notion of being categorized or typecast, though they readily grasped and greatly enjoyed discussing the Ryan Theory of Adolescent Development in American Males as it applies to all other players. The aura of mystery that surrounded them when they played organized youth baseball persists throughout their lives. This, too, is a preference and a matter of choice.

13

The Right Fielder

In the outfield, fly balls are my only weakness.   —*Carmelo Martinez*

Ingredients

At Griffin's Bar in Holyoke, Massachusetts, a contest was conducted one night to determine the worst of all possible curses. These were the winners in descending order:

10. May your tongue swell till you bite it at every meal.
9. May you spend your life savings on chemotherapy.
8. May you catch gonorrhea from your wife.
7. May all your children be lawyers.
6. May your granddaughter be featured on a carton of milk.
5. May you have diarrhea until the Red Sox win a World Series.

4. May your mother-in-law move in with you until the Cubs win a pennant.
3. May your bartender run out of beer.
2. May you develop an allergy to beer.
1. May you sire a right fielder.

For a man, there is only one thing in life worse than being a right fielder: being a right fielder's father. Fortunately, if that happens you probably wouldn't know it. No child who has had the slightest contact with an adult male has ever become a right fielder. Right fielders are born, bred, raised, and reared solely by their mothers. Many never even leave the confines of their domiciles until that fateful day when their mothers drag them, kicking and screaming, to baseball tryouts. It's easier to give a dog a bath than to get a right fielder to volunteer to play baseball. Instinctively, they know it's a natural predator that will devour them.

As with other players, there are simple tests for early identification of right fielders. Observe the kids as they arrive for tryouts. Is there a woman dragging a child from the car by his ankles? Does he claw the ground like a rabid animal, scream like a banshee, kick like a snared rabbit? Is he wearing a beanie with a propeller on top? That's the right fielder.

If you arrive after the wannabes, observe the kids playing pepper. Is there one who falls down when he tries to catch or throw or run or stand in line? That's the right fielder.

If you arrive still later, observe the children at fielding practice. Is there one so inept, clumsy, and spastic that you realize he has the glove on the wrong hand? Tell him to switch the glove. If his performance improves remarkably, he's a third baseman. If there's no change, he's a right fielder.

If you arrive in the middle of tryouts, meander over to hitting practice, where a YBC is lobbing balls underhand to observe how the batters take their cuts. Does one of them grip the bat at the wrong end? At the approach of the ball, does he drop the bat and run to a fat woman wearing a party dress and apron? Or does he wet his pants and start to cry? If the answer to any of these questions is affirmative, you have been watching a born right fielder.

This may sound cruel. If so, it's an unintended consequence of speaking the truth because there is no way to honestly describe a right fielder without sounding cruel. Besides, right fielders are accustomed to it. Life itself is so cruel to right fielders that all would become serial killers except they lack the coordination and dexterity that murder requires.

Right fielders have two left feet, two left hands, and two left eyes. Uncoordinated people are reputed to be unable to walk and chew gum simultaneously. Right fielders can't do either without getting hurt. Clumsy people trip on their shoelaces and timid people are afraid of their own shadows. Right fielders are afraid of their shoelaces and trip on their own shadows.

Right fielders are the last kids chosen on teams but every team ends up with one. Their mothers come to every game, cheer for every kid who comes to the plate, and hand out cookies and Kool-Aid afterward. Every right fielder misses five games a year, two from sunburn, two from poison ivy, and one as a punishment for wetting his bed. It's only one game for bedwetting because his mother quickly catches on that he's purposely pissing in the sheets to avoid the games.

Right fielders have no father, grandfather, uncle, brother, cousin, or friend to play catch with. Their mothers attempt to teach them the rudiments of the game so all their lives they will throw like girls.

No matter what the space between the right fielder and the person he is throwing to, the vertical flight of the ball will always be at least four times the horizontal. Frequently, when he attempts a long throw, the ball will go straight up and land on his head when it comes down. Many right fielders have damaged the little propellers on their caps in this manner, an occurrence that always brings tears to the little fellow's eyes.

The Mold

Organized youth baseball is as unforgettable as it is miserable for right fielders. Indeed, the psychological scars will be permanent. Put a kid in right field at eight years old and he'll have nightmares when he's eighty. Wherever he goes, whatever he does, whoever he is, teammates will remember him as a right fielder. In fact, he will be instantly recognized by strangers as a former right fielder. Some will be sympathetic, others merciful, a few venomous, but all aware. Hester Prynne's scarlet letter was less noticeable than the imprint right field leaves on a person's psyche.

It's not the conduct of a right fielder that marks him for life but the mere fact of being a right fielder. Not counting the foul balls he is required to retrieve, a right fielder will be expected to touch a baseball only five times in the course of an entire youth baseball season. Three of these will be ground balls that hug the foul line and die in the grass behind the first baseman. These being too far right for the center fielder and too deep for the first baseman or the second baseman who is backing him up, the right fielder must waddle to it as fast as his spindly legs will carry him, pick it up, and wiggle his way to the nearest player without dropping it. Right fielders are under strict orders not to attempt to throw a ball during a game under any circumstances. They are instructed to run it in and hand it over.

This is the opposite of the standard operating procedure for every other position and one of the right fielder's distinguishing exceptions to the general rules. The other two occasions when contact with the baseball is expected of right fielders are when fly balls are hit directly at them. They are instructed to position themselves immediately next to the foul line so that they will not obstruct the center fielder's pursuit of all fair fly balls, but twice a year balls will come right at them and they must do something.

This is where another of the right fielder's distinguishing exceptions to the general rules comes into play. Everyone else is instructed to "get under the ball!" The right fielder is warned to get away from it so he doesn't get hurt. He is told to back up so the ball falls in front of him and not to let it roll past him into the poison ivy. He is to pick it up, hold it with two hands, and run it in to the nearest player.

The right fielder will fail in one of his attempts to stop the ball from reaching the poison ivy. When the ball rolls into the patch, he'll stop at the edge. The center fielder will arrive moments afterward, punch him in the stomach, call him a name, and send him in after the ball.

This will mean the batter has hit a home run but somebody is going to break out in a rash, and the center fielder doesn't want to be the somebody. Neither does the right fielder but he has little choice. It's either a rash or a black eye, and itching is more tolerable than aching. Besides, after retrieving the ball he can skip the next two games and stay home covered in calamine lotion.

To the stigma of being a right fielder is added the insult of the distinguishing exceptions to the general rules. Two have been explained. There is a third. The right fielder always bats ninth, and when he goes to the plate, the YBC tells him, "Don't swing. Maybe you'll draw a walk." That's it. That's what makes a right fielder. He's playing baseball and has three special instructions that apply only to him:

1. Don't try to catch the ball,
2. Don't try to throw the ball, and
3. Don't try to hit the ball.

A funny thing happens to the right fielder once in his baseball career, usually in his last game. A fly ball is hit in his direction. He has not been paying attention but is alerted to his predicament by the cries of his teammates. He sticks his glove in the air to protect his head and starts backpedaling to safety.

Something strikes his glove, knocking him ass over elbows in a somersault. He is dazed and dizzy but when he can focus his eyes, he finds the baseball secure in the webbing of his glove. His hand hurts and he may never be able to play baseball again, but what a finale to his brief and painful career.

The center fielder is first on the scene and alerts everyone with his whoop of shock that the ball was caught. The second baseman comes to witness the miracle. He is followed by the shortstop, the first baseman, and the pitcher. The umpire has to see for himself and the YBC jogs out to keep the ump honest. So do the other YBC and the kid who clobbered the ball. All kneel down to see for themselves, and when the right fielder struggles to his feet he feels like King Arthur of the Round Table rising victorious from a field of battle, surrounded by his homage-paying knights. For one brief and shining moment, there is Camelot.

The Finished Product

It's the mark of Cain, a curse on generations to come. Right fielders have their own group therapy sessions. There is a twelve-step program for recovering right fielders. Two thirds of the males in America without issue who undergo vasectomies played right field in youth baseball. In a recent survey of all first-year baseball players in Texas, not one admitted being descended from a right fielder.

Only 5 percent of right fielders live as adults in the towns where they played youth baseball. Sperm banks refuse donations from only two groups, paranoid schizophrenics and right fielders. When this survey was conducted, only twenty-seven right fielders consented to personal interviews and all wore paper bags covering their heads. The other six hundred eleven would answer questions only over the telephone and all stipulated the interview be anonymous.

Right fielders abhor baseball. Recently a man in California who had twenty-four hours to present a winning lottery ticket in Florida disembarked his airplane in Chicago because *Bull Durham* was scheduled to be the in-flight movie. Investigative reporters discovered he was a former right fielder. Forty percent of the NASA volunteers for the Year in Space program were screened out because their sole reason for volunteering was to go to a place where baseball wasn't played. Ditto for applications to the observation camp at the North Pole, the French Foreign Legion, and New York's Bellevue Hospital.

Right fielders who are competitive play bridge; those who like spectator sports choose figure skating twelve to one over all games involving a ball of any size, shape, or dimensions, even if it's called a puck, a shuttlecock, or a birdie. When asked their favorite games of youth, they list ring-around-the-rosy, hide-and-seek, and spelling bees.

Right fielders are not distinguishable by intellect and cover the same IQ spectrum as any randomly selected group. There is no discernible pattern of material or professional success or failure, nor any clustering in particular occupations. Here, too, they run the gamut.

What patterns emerge from isolation of right fielders as a subgroup are primarily social and psychological. Right fielders suffer a high rate of post-traumatic stress syndrome; matricide is rare in this culture but occurs seven times more frequently among former right fielders than among samples of the general population. In at least one case, the defense was justifiable homicide based on the mother's forcing the child to play organized youth baseball. However, as we go to print, this "Battered Right Fielder's Defense" has not yet been accepted in most jurisdictions.

Right fielders avoid all groups of men and spurn memberships in civic organizations such as the Rotary, Lions, and Kiwanis, as well as labor unions, fraternal organizations such as the Eagles and Elks, rod and gun clubs, the YMCA, country clubs, and posses. Right fielders refuse to hunt or fish and never hang out in bars, taverns, or saloons.

Anywhere where men gather, the subject of baseball is likely to arise, and right fielders break out in hives, retch, and develop stutters at the mere mention of the subject.

Right fielders of wealth travel to Europe during the World Series, avoid Florida during spring training, and call in sick on opening day. The difference between them and everybody else who claimed to be ailing is that they really are sick. Right fielders establish themselves in cities that have no major or minor league baseball teams and will not read newspapers from such cities from April to November. They go to bed at ten o'clock to avoid hearing the news during baseball season.

Right fielders make devoted husbands who spend their leisure hours close to home. They prefer not to live in houses with lawns, as green grass nauseates them, but if they must, they will hire a neighborhood kid to mow the front and install a patio or pool that covers the entire backyard. They detest country living due to their deep fear of poison ivy. Their ideal domicile is a high-rise apartment or condominium in a baseball-less metropolis.

In romance, right fielders are hesitant, shy, timid, and indecisive. They lack self-confidence and self-esteem. Fifty percent of married right fielders were proposed to by their wives, 10 percent of their marriages were arranged by their mothers, 10 percent obtained mail order brides from overseas, and another 5 percent were married on blind dates with illegal aliens desperate to stay in this country. Eighty-five percent preferred fatherless women without brothers.

As fathers, right fielders are loving but overprotective and prefer daughters to sons until they reach dating age. Then they would rather see their daughters date and marry members of gangs than members of teams. Given a choice between a son who plays baseball and a son who sniffs glue, they'll keep the lad supplied with plastic model airplanes and all the accessories, knowing in their heart of hearts that such an addiction is less harmful than the trauma of being labeled a right fielder.

Right fielders are among the kindest and most charitable of our citizens. Many work hard for equality and justice on local, state, and federal levels and promote harmony among the nations of the world. Peacemakers are overwhelmingly ex–right fielders, as are a high percentage of arbitrators, negotiators, and mediators.

A right fielder is particularly kind to the physically impaired and often volunteers to work with disabled children. As he wheels his little charge about the hospital grounds, he encourages him or her to have hope and hints that when he was a child, he too was severely handicapped. Without revealing the exact nature of his malady, he'll describe his feeble attempt to participate in organized sports and describe his one feat of heroics in a reverent, hushed tone.

When he finishes, the child will be very still and after a long pause will look up to see tears in the old right fielder's eyes.

"Are you crying?" the child will whisper.

"Yes," will come his reply.

"You must have been a right fielder."

It's the mark of Cain. Those right fielders, they can't fool anybody, not even a kid.

14

Substitutes, Batboys, and Nonplayers

You can't get rich sitting on the bench—but I'm giving it a try.

—*Phil Linz*

I hate all sports as rabidly as a person who likes sports hates common sense.

—*H. L. Mencken*

Substitutes

Not everybody makes the first team. Every team has three extra players since league commissioners like an even dozen players on each roster. Eleven is too few, fourteen is too many, and thirteen is unlucky. All baseball players are superstitious and no roster has ever contained thirteen players. Fourteen is too many because five kids—the pitcher, the first baseman, the center fielder, the second baseman, and the shortstop—must play the entire game. These five are essential to the team's chances for victory. The other four never affect the game's outcome but it's fitting and proper to have left fielders, third basemen, catchers, and right fielders so that baseball can be all-inclusive and provide competitive opportunities for everyone. League rules require each kid play a minimum of three innings, so with three substitutes, every team has alternates for 75 percent of its useless players.

The essential five never miss a game or practice but the worthless four are habitually absent or tardy. Left fielders skip for recitals, right fielders come down with poison ivy, third basemen forget times and dates, and catchers have doctor appointments. That's why eleven is too few and twelve is ideal.

The best substitutes combine the qualities of two or more positions, but there is such a canyon between left fielders and third basemen that no sub can be an all-around utility player.

The two most common substitutes are fat space shots, who can play catcher or left field, and stupid geeks, who can fill in at third base or right field. Lucky is the YBC who can fill his roster with a chubby, witless spaz who is equally adept at being unproductive in right field, at the hot corner, and behind the plate.

Substitutes generally exhibit the limitations and foibles of the person they replace, but have an added dimension that renders them even more useless than the starter. It takes a discerning eye to detect the relative weaknesses of two inept players, and only the most experienced YBC can choose starters and substitutes at the worthless positions with any degree of accuracy.

There's little accountability because there's no consequence to the YBC for misjudgments. A YBC's won-lost record is not diminished because his starting third baseman missed a ground ball by eighteen inches and he had a guy on the bench who could have missed it by a foot. If a YBC guesses wrong on his first-team useless player, the starter strikes out on three pitches when it would have taken the fellow cheated out of the starting role five. A lot of YBCs confronted with this type of data say, "So what?"

Well, it means a lot to the kid, that's so what. It's ego-deflating enough to be a starting right fielder. How much lower will a backup feel years later when the relief of not playing wears off? And can anyone imagine how bitter it makes a kid feel to watch a third baseman run to the wrong base while he sits idle knowing in his heart he could have run to the wrong base a lot faster? Even though these decisions are inconsequential, a responsible YBC agonizes over them.

Substitute left fielders are spared much of the trauma of not making the first team because they don't notice, particularly if the team's bench has dandelions around it or the floor of the dugout has ants. In either case, there's plenty to do and the call to enter the game is often a source of irritation and aggravation.

There are little tricks of the trade that the experienced YBC employs to ease the pain of rejection. He can tell the substitute third baseman and right fielder that they are secret weapons and the YBC wants to lull the other YBC into a false sense of security before he deploys them. The third baseman will believe this and think his YBC a most clever fellow. The right fielder will not believe it, but his assignment on the bench will be an answer to his prayers and he will spend the first half of the game being quiet and nondescript in hopes he will be forgotten in the second half as well.

If a YBC has two catchers, it's good to have two sets of catcher's gear. That way, as soon as the game starts he can hustle over to the substitute and tell him he should have been starting and he'll be in the game as soon as he gets his gear on. This project will take the backup catcher four innings, so by the time he's ready it's time to send him in.

At least two of the subs will miss every game after the first one, so subbing is not a major problem. Sometimes the biggest difficulty, even with a roster of twelve, is fielding a full nine-person team. That's why it's always good to have a batboy.

Batboys

Batboys are younger brothers of the second baseman or younger sons of the YBC. Sometimes they are the children of the YBC's girlfriend. However they were chosen, it was not because of any innate talent or precocious aptitude for baseball. Batboys wear the same uniform as the players but come in smaller sizes.

They are like irritating mongrel dogs who like to play fetch and keep dropping saliva-logged tennis balls at your feet. They roam around with an oversized glove and a hat that covers their face and repeat seven times a second, "Wanna play catch?"

Batboys have mothers with cameras who, due to childhood diseases or other tragic misfortunes that no one talks about, have vocabularies of only three words. Like the voice alarms on the latest-model luxury cars, these three words are automatically spoken if a human being approaches within several feet of them. See a woman with a camera at a baseball game? Walk up beside her. A prerecorded voice sighs, "Isn't he cute?" That woman is the batboy's mother.

From the YBC to the substitute right fielder, every person who enters the foul lines has to have his picture taken with the batboy. Most often the camera is a Polaroid. As soon as the murky image emerges from the base of the camera, the mother coos, "Isn't he cute?"

Within a week of the picture taking, the person who humored the batboy's mom receives a copy of the picture in a pink envelope that smells like the Avon Lady's sample case. The accompanying note reads, "Save this for your scrapbook and you can impress your friends when little Johnny is famous." All the i's are dotted with little hearts, it's signed "Little Johnny's Mom," and has xoxoxo under the signature.

The batboy kneels next to the on deck circle, chases foul balls, and picks up the bat dropped by the hitter. He loves it when a ball gets by the catcher because the little bugger can then charge after the ball and without much effort beat the catcher to it, pick it up, and heave it back in the air to the pitcher. This really antagonizes the catcher. Someone in the stands always comments that the little tyke has a great arm and should be playing. This is a signal for the mom and she responds as programmed: "Isn't he cute?"

Catchers are not the only players who resent batboys. In fact, the one and only trait that all the players have in common is that they all hate the batboy. He's a know-it-all, strike one; a tattletale, strike two; and a crybaby, strike three. Whenever a player strikes out, the batboy will run up to him, ostensibly to relieve him of the lumber, but really to explain what he did wrong.

The player, after being told by a shrimp about half his size that he's a sucker for high ones, bats with his foot in the bucket, or needs glasses, expresses his appreciation for the batboy's insight by kicking the pipsqueak's butt. The batboy lets out a whoop and runs to the YBC crying that he was just trying to help out and got kicked in the arse.

The YBC suppresses his secret approval of this vigilante justice and tells the kicker to apologize. As soon as the kid does, the batboy sniffles and says, "Wanna play catch?" An alert YBC sends the erstwhile batter behind the dugout to play catch with the batboy, thereby simultaneously punishing the player appropriately and getting the batboy out of his hair.

When batters hit the ball and commence their excursion to first base, they frequently throw their bats. The bat twirls toward the on deck hitter like a disconnected helicopter blade, causing alarm, trepidation, and panic. It is a dangerous habit and frequently causes concussions, broken noses, and deep bruises. YBCs have preached, cursed, and warned for years without diminishing the frequency of batters throwing their bats, but there is one sure cure. Get rid of the batboy.

Studies have shown that when batboys are banished, the incidence of bat throwing almost entirely disappears. It is improbable that most bat throwings are deliberate attempts of felonious assault on batboys, but the urge to do them physical harm is a powerful subconscious drive and undoubtedly accounts for a significant proportion of the twirling bats.

Most batboys survive and go on to play organized youth baseball, in which case there are no lasting effects. Still, you can always tell a former batboy when watching the game from the bleachers. No matter what position he plays and no matter what he accomplishes or attempts, every time he does anything, a proud, syrupy voice chirps from the stands, "Isn't he cute?"

Nonplayers

In some impoverished sections of this great nation, there is no organized youth baseball. Some young lads, for reasons of family circumstances or perverted social values, decide not to play organized youth baseball when the opportunity is there. It makes no difference why a particular eight-year-old does not play, because in the long run the effect is the same: alienation.

No male who did not play baseball as a child ever feels like a full-blooded American. Whenever and wherever men gather, baseball eventually becomes the topic of conversation and the nonplayers are made to feel like outsiders, outlaws, and strangers among their gender peers. Nonplayers feel isolated whenever they hear "The Star-Spangled Banner," particularly if it's being played on an organ. Whenever someone orders a hot dog, they cringe. Whenever a baseball term is used, they blush. Whenever they see a man in uniform, their stomachs growl. Whenever the evening news reaches the baseball scores, they feel intestinal pressure to fart. Any reminder of baseball is threatening.

All this derives from fear of exposure as a nonplayer and is based on years of public humiliations. A boy does not grow to manhood in the United States without being asked on numerous occasions, "What position did you play?" To the reply, "I didn't play," comes the incredulous question, "Why not?"

In response, nonplayers lie. Some claim a childhood illness, some assert that they grew up at the North Pole. A few claim to have been shipwrecked as toddlers and raised by South Pacific islanders. The worst whopper is to claim to have played, because the nonplayer is instantly exposed as a liar. No one can fake being a catcher, shortstop, center fielder, or any other position, because he will not have the identifying marks and real players will instinctively see through the charade.

Alienation targets the stomach. A marketing survey by a large pharmaceutical firm in the Midwest recently revealed that 77 percent of men who purchase antacids more than twice a week did not play baseball in their formative years. Patient profiles at a major New York City medical center, which cannot be disclosed for reasons of patient confidentiality, confirmed that over 50 percent of the men in their twenties and thirties who underwent surgery for ulcers were non–baseball players.

There is an authentic basis for these stomach difficulties. The cause is not imaginary. Americans are hesitant to trust a man who never stood at the plate and took his swings. President Eisenhower spoke for the nation when he said, "Never trust a man who didn't play baseball." According to still unreleased secret tapes, when the nonplayer John Dean III turned state's evidence and began testifying before Sam Ervin's Watergate Committee, Richard Nixon broke down and sobbed, "I should have listened to Ike."

Benedict Arnold, the most famous traitor in American history, never saw a ball field in his youth. Nathan Hale, on the other hand, played "second post" for the New Haven Rebels in the Connecticut Colonial Rounders League while attending Yale. Disloyalty is common among nonplayers. Sixty-nine percent of the informants in the federal witness protection program are nonplayers.

It was Will Rogers who said, "I never met a baseball player I didn't like." Every American elected president after Ulysses S.

Grant was a former baseball player, even Harry Truman, who overcame childhood illnesses and poor eyesight to play an occasional right field in Kansas cornfield pickup games.

The CIA has an unwritten regulation that any male who did not play baseball cannot be sent undercover in a foreign country or given access to the identity of such agents. Henry Ford would not consider nonplayers for managerial positions in his automotive company, and one national fast food restaurant chain will not sell a franchise to a nonplayer. This discrimination is very subtle and seldom openly discussed. In fact, it's so well hidden that no civil rights lawsuits have yet been filed, but the prejudice permeates and plagues the life of nonplayers.

There are two extreme reactions to baseball-induced alienation common to all nonplayers. Either they completely drop out of society to avoid confronting the bias against them or they totally immerse themselves in the culture of sports to overcome their deficiency. This explains why 40 percent of adult males who collect baseball cards and autographs of major leaguers were nonplayers. And then there's Howard Cosell, who wrote his autobiographical admission, *I Never Played the Game*.

Fifty-six percent of the owners of sports bars and baseball souvenir shops were also nonplayers. The numbers rise to over 90 percent if the establishment is called the Dugout or the Bullpen, the choice of name being a subconscious confession of being on the sidelines and not involved in the action.

Other nonplayers become diplomats, foreign correspondents, explorers, archaeologists, and managers of rubber-tree plantations. In the locations that these men live and work, they encounter few ex-ballplayers, and those with whom they do interact have been right fielders, who do not talk about baseball, and left fielders, who have few memories of actually playing the grand old game. Those who remain in the continental United States take up birdwatching as a hobby and frequently work in solitary occupations, such as computer programming.

Nonplayers are normally law-abiding citizens and very few resort to a life of crime. This is because prisons in America are gender-segregated and confinement means discussions of baseball and eventual exposure as a nonplayer. No one wants to be revealed as untrustworthy when doing time.

Women who become romantically involved with nonplayers may be pleased that their beloved is a homebody but should be aware that there is an ever-present danger of desertion. The unsolved mystery of Judge Crater's disappearance was right under the investigator's nose. The last man known to have seen him on the street recounted that nothing seemed unusual, they simply discussed the weather and the previous day's Highlanders game. Judge Crater never played baseball and that conversation was the straw that broke his back. He fled to a land where baseball did not exist.

It would be a major step toward resolving most missing persons reports if police investigators would be trained to ask the obvious question, "Did Mr. X play baseball when he was a kid?" If the answer is affirmative, the police are justified in suspecting foul play, whereas a negative reply conclusively establishes a motive for voluntarily disappearing.

For those who desire a litmus test to determine if an associate played baseball, the following is offered:

Invite the suspect to lunch. Bring a companion, arrive early, and select a table in a quiet corner without an easy escape. Ideally, pick a booth and manipulate the seating when the suspect arrives so that he is blocked in by you or your companion. As he sits, announce that you were just discussing the proposed "three strikes and you're out" legislation. Does his lower lip tremble? When the waitress arrives, order hot dogs. Does a rash appear above his collar? When the victuals arrive, comment that the best hot dogs in America are Fenway franks. Does sweat break out on his forehead?

You have now destroyed his natural defenses. He is vulnerable; go for the jugular. In unison, you and the third party begin singing "Take Me Out to the Ball Game." If he's a player, he'll join in. If he never picked up a glove, he'll break wind before you intone, "I don't care if we never get back."

It's a cruel and grueling test, but it's 100 percent accurate and sometimes necessary. After all, everyone in this world occasionally needs to know if a person can be trusted with secrets of state. If George Washington had given this test to Benedict Arnold, he would not have put him in charge of West Point. If Richard Nixon had put it to John Dean III, he would have had a longer stay at 1600 Pennsylvania Avenue; if Pete Rose had used it to check out his bookie, he'd be in the Hall of Fame today.

While it is often detrimental to the development of self-esteem in American adolescent males to play organized youth baseball, there is something even more perilous: not playing organized youth baseball.

15

Batting Orders

Managing is getting paid for the home runs someone else hits.

—*Casey Stengel*

Whichever team scores the most runs wins the game, and in America winning is what counts. Hence the importance of scoring, as an end unto itself, is apparent. You don't score, you don't win; you don't win, you don't count. If you want to count, you have to win; if you want to win, you have to score. Batting orders are chosen with a single view and for a single purpose: scoring.

Certain universal principles apply to youth baseball and govern YBCs' decisions in establishing the team batting order. Each YBC thinks he's the only one who knows them and also thinks he has a winning edge because of this unique knowledge. The reality is that every YBC knows them and that's why they all end up with the same batting order. As noted previously, there are few geniuses in baseball.

Just as an appreciation of theater requires a willing suspension of disbelief, an enjoyment of playing baseball requires a willing suspension of intellect. This is most important when walking to the plate and digging into the batter's box. These are the realities that govern batting order determinations:

1. A baseball is hard.
2. If a moving baseball hits you, it hurts.
3. The faster a baseball moves, the more it hurts.
4. Human instinct dictates avoidance of things that hurt.
5. Human experience teaches avoidance of things that hurt.
6. It is insane and unwise to stand in a batter's box and let someone throw baseballs at you.
7. To hit the ball, you must stay in the batter's box.
8. Therefore, to hit the ball you must be stupid or crazy.
9. Since all baseball players are stupid, the best batter is the craziest.

Universally, the craziest kid on the team is the shortstop, which is why the shortstop is always the leadoff batter. What is bizarre is the common judgment of YBCs and the usual comments of spectators concerning leadoff hitters.

Some eight-year-old, seventy-two-pound, four-foot ten-inch shortstop steps into the box, digs in, and doesn't jump back when a thirty-mile-an-hour fastball zooms by his head and everybody agrees the kid is "a natural." He is not! In fact, the number nine hitter who backs up to the on deck circle when the pitcher starts his windup is the natural; he is the end product of two million years of nature's survival-of-the-smartest process.

Given the natural propensity of fielders to dodge hard-hit balls (see hard and fast principles one through four above), leadoff batters commonly reach first base safely. When one does, it becomes the role of the number two batter to move the base runner along. It is more than a responsibility, it is a duty. The quality required is dependability. The YBC looks for someone who will stand in and take the inside pitch on the rump; someone who will lay down the sacrifice bunt; someone who will, when ordered, take six straight pitches in hopes of a walk. There's an easy way to determine the team's number two hitter. He's the kid who stands at attention with his hat over his heart during the national anthem. That's right, the one who will do his duty to God, country, and team. The Boy Scout. Nine out of ten times the number two hitter is the second baseman. The tenth time, it's the YBC's son and the second baseman bats in the number seven slot.

The players in slots three, four, and five are the biggest kids on the team, excluding the right fielder. The right fielder is a klutz. He might be a big klutz or a little klutz. It doesn't matter. He will always bat ninth and always strike out looking. If the right fielder does swing the bat, the catcher has already caught the ball. Once or twice a season a right fielder will draw a walk or be struck by a pitch, but those are the only ways he'll ever see first base.

Walking the right fielder is the greatest disgrace a pitcher can suffer but there are no lasting consequences. After the pitcher is thoroughly berated by the YBC and taunted by the opposing players, the first baseman will walk to the mound, console the pitcher, stash the ball in his glove, and return to his position. When the right fielder daringly takes a nine-inch lead off first base, the first baseman will tag him out. This hidden ball trick works only on right fielders, but on right fielders it works every time. This is another example of a mystery out which occurs too rarely to be accurately predicted.

Incidentally, in the history of youth baseball, only two right fielders have ever reached second base and both were so lost and confused they ran back to first when the next batter hit the ball.

Enough about right fielders/ninth batters. There is little in the way of batting skill to distinguish the third, fourth, and fifth batters in the order. All are relatively tall, strong, and competitive. Macho types. They are not as crazy as number one or as reliable as number two, but they fancy themselves as stronger.

They won't step away from fastballs like batters six, seven, and eight, but they will, when frightened, swing the big swing and let their momentum pull them away from the plate and out of harm's way. When the YBC calls out, "Don't try to kill it, just meet it," you know the batter chickened out and got away with it.

Both the third and fifth think they should be number four. If the fourth batter's father is the YBC, one of them is right. While the exact order varies, these three positions are always filled by the pitcher, the first baseman, and the center fielder. Their role is to hit the ball into the outfield, preferably to right field. Any ball that goes over the first baseman's head is considered right field and guarantees a home run.

The number four hitter always hates the number three hitter. This is because number four is the cleanup batter and feels cheated if no one is on base when he steps to the plate. Number four hitters have someone watching, usually a parent, mother type, who is keeping track of their RBIs. They are typically entitled to a dollar or an ice-cream cone for each RBI.

The number three hitter sometimes ends the inning with an out, but more often hits a Kodak home run. Either way, there is no one on base when the cleanup batter steps in, and over the course of a season the third batter will cost him up to twenty gallons of ice cream or a down payment on a pair of Nikes for basketball season. That's why number four hates number three.

Number five is the best friend of both three and four. He secretly enjoys three striking out or clearing the bases because it's more likely four will be on base for him to drive home. On the other hand, when four does hit the homer, he, as the on deck hitter, gets the first high-five. Reflected glory, it's called.

Batters six, seven, and eight are the favorites of the grandparents, aunts and uncles, and brothers and sisters of the first five batters, who are socially obligated to attend the games but want them to end quickly. These kids oblige: they produce the outs. Odds are that six is the left fielder. He is likely as good a natural hitter as anyone on the team but he questions the wisdom of remaining in the batter's box and steps away from the pitch as he swings. If the YBC yells, "Ya put yer foot in the bucket," the batter is number six and the left fielder.

Number seven is the third baseman. He, too, is afraid of the ball. Unlike the left fielder, however, his fear is not based on the rational deduction that the ball will hurt. He is a Neanderthal and his fear is instinctive, but he will do what the YBC tells him to do. He will plant his feet and not move them. He will not step backward from a speeding ball. Instead, he leans backward from the waist and falls on his ass. When you see a ballplayer with a round ring of dirt on his rump, he's a third baseman and he bats seventh in the order.

Six and seven typically strike out a lot. They only swing at outside pitches and when they connect it's on the tip of the bat, producing slow rollers to the right side of the infield, easy pickings for the first or second baseman. Occasionally, the sixth or seventh will close his eyes on an inside pitch and the ball will hit near the grip. These balls roll harmlessly to the pitcher who underhands them softly to his pal at first base.

The catcher bats eighth. He is short, heavy, and slow of foot. He's the only kid on the team who can smack a ball into center field and still be thrown out at first. No catcher, even one with the power to pull one over the napping left fielder's head, has ever hit a triple or home run. Catchers simply lack the stamina to run that far. The few who have tried collapsed breathless around the shortstop's position and were tagged out trying to crawl back to second.

As stated earlier, right fielders always bat ninth. Only a mother comes to watch the ninth batter play. She spends the entire inning praying for seven or eight to make the last out to spare her child the humiliation. It's so much easier to make the first or second out than the last one. When a number nine does get up to bat with two outs, the catcher puts on his shin guards, chest protector, and mask and the other players pick up their gloves and start their stretching exercises. There was a report that once, around 1967, a number nine batter came up with two outs and one of his teammates actually watched him try to hit, but this could not be confirmed and the story is retold only to demonstrate the wild imaginations of children.

While the decision of who shall hit where in the order may seem capricious, particularly when deciding on three, four, and five or between seven and eight, the decision has lifelong consequences. To understand this, a quick review of the situation is warranted.

Customarily, in the United States of America, baseball is an adolescent male's first experience with organized competition. It is the first occasion that the young boy is evaluated, judged, rated, and ranked by adult males from outside his kin group. An increasing number of such boys come from single-parent households and attend elementary schools that employ only female teachers. Thus the YBC often becomes the first adult male to recognize and acknowledge the child's existence.

In such circumstances, the YBC's attitude toward the youth will have the force and impact of a tribal judgment. The impression will be burned into the child's subconscious mind like a brand of a ranch on the hind end of a calf. The youth himself will adopt the YBC's assessment as his lifelong self-image. It is indelible, unchangeable, permanent.

A sensitive YBC can send a chubby, clumsy little munchkin to right field and tell him that he's doing something important, that the team is depending on him, and that the coaching staff has great confidence in him. The understanding YBC can give the child an easy assignment like, "Don't let the ball roll into the poison ivy."

When the kid trots back to the bench after watching six grounders reach the highway and four pop-ups land at his feet, this sensitive and understanding YBC can pat the boy on the back and say, "Great job at keeping the ball out of the poison ivy, kid. Keep it up and you'll be the next Willie Mays." There it is, affirmation. Validation. Another potential psycho-killer deterred from rampage and pillage.

However, let this same Mr. Roberts kind of coach put the same kid at the number nine slot in his batting order and no matter how moronic and clueless the twit be, he'll figure out he's scum in a tub. Numbers one, two, and four will thrive; three and five will survive but the bitterness of not being four will gnaw at their innards as long as they live. Number six will get by with minor damage to his self-respect by discussing the matter thoroughly with his therapist. Number seven is too dumb to notice the insult and number eight's embarrassment will be mollified by his relief that he's not nine. He will befriend nine and try to keep him happy so he'll remain on the team. Without nine, eight is dog vomit and knows it.

The position a player is assigned in the field dictates his development of personality but his place in the batting order (PIBO) determines his sense of self-worth.

Nowhere is the consequence of PIBO more apparent than in the course of a male youth's sexual maturation. Survey results of former youth baseball players who reached puberty in the '60s, '70s, and '80s reveal that PIBO is reliable with mathematical precision as a predictor of sexual development. While the exact methodology of the study must remain confidential, let it be noted here that renowned sexologists have examined our procedures and deemed them flawless.

Among the findings of our panel of experts are the following:

A. PIBO equals the order that the players will develop their interest in girls.

B. PIBO equals the number of times a player will ask a girl out before he stops asking.

C. PIBO equals the number of girls a player will ask out before one says yes.

D. PIBO equals the number of dates a former player will have before he expects to get to first base.

E. PIBO equals the additional dates a former player will have before he gets to second base, third base, and home.

F. PIBO reversed (1=9, 2=8, 3=7, 4=6) equals the number of girls a player will date before he asks one to go steady.

G. Between any two players, the inverse ratio of their PIBOs equals the ratio of their total number of dates in high school. (For example, the number one shortstop will have nine times as many as the number nine right fielder.)

There are many other effects of PIBO on a player's sexual maturation, but this is not the right forum in which to reveal them.

PIBO is also a solid indicator of a player's future success in the employment market. PIBO equals the number of job applications a former player will fill out before receiving an interview; the number of job interviews a former player will attend before being hired; the number of times a former player will request a raise before receiving one; and the number of times a former player can expect to be discharged or laid off during the course of his career.

A player's PIBO will be a lifelong talisman. It will always be the number he picks when he has to pick a number between one and ten. His license plate, passport, and social security number will either start or end with his PIBO. It will be the number of times he has to call his dog to get it to stop biting the mailman and the number of places he has to call for a dinner, hotel, or rental car reservation at the last minute. It will be the number of times he has to circle the block to find a parking space, the number of places he has to look to find his car keys, wallet, or umbrella, the number of extras he likes on his pizza, and the number of resolutions he makes every New Year's Eve.

PIBO reversed is an accurate predictor of the number of ushers a player will have at his first wedding, the number of rooms a player will have in his home at age forty, the number of motor vehicles a player will own in any ten-year period, the number of sports a player will take up seriously after youth baseball, the number of New Year's resolutions a player will keep in the course of his life, and the number of former teammates who will attend his funeral.

Between any two players, the ratio of their PIBOs will reflect the odds of their being mugged in New York City, bumped from an airline on their vacation, called to jury duty for a nineteen-week trial, having their in-laws move in permanently, or accepting a counterfeit twenty from the grocery store clerk. The higher one batted in the order, the luckier and happier his future life will be.

Once the public understands the full impact of PIBO, it is only a matter of time before lawyers start suing YBCs for PIBO malpractice and intentional infliction of emotional distress. YBCs would be wise to consult their local insurance representatives or family lawyers before selecting their batting orders.

16

The PIF Theory of Group Dynamics

Baseball holds the secret to the national character.

—*Michael Novack*

Any group whose members habitually interact can be divided into subgroups based on position-in-the-field (PIF) personalities. No group with fewer than nine members will have two members in the same subgroup. Our data establishes this proposition but unfortunately cannot prove it. Indeed, unless every group in the universe were examined, proof is impossible. Field testing of this proposition has supported the preliminary findings, however, and anecdotal evidence of accuracy is substantial enough to proffer it as a theory.

Examples of two groups well known in popular culture are presented here to demonstrate the theory in practice. The first example is the Kennedy clan.

The patriarch, Joseph Kennedy Sr., was an Irish-born Bostonian who grew up feeling second rate and second best in Brahmin-controlled Massachusetts. Frustrated, he left for New York to make his fortune and prove the damn Yankees wrong. He was a first baseman.

His firstborn was named Joseph Jr., and the father coached and guided the namesake to be the first Catholic president of the United States. Joe Jr. was handsome, athletic, charming, and had a flair for claiming center stage. He was a pitcher.

Jack Kennedy had much potential as a youth but was your basic underachiever, at least until Joe perished in World War II. He marched to the tune of his own drummer, relished poetry, studied philosophy, appreciated classical music and the arts, was oblivious to parental pressure, and loved the ambiance of the world (i.e., the seas, flowers, wide open spaces, stars, and thunderstorms). He was a left fielder.

For reasons explained in the text, Bobby Kennedy was a bona fide shortstop.

Teddy, the youngest, was a roly-poly youth who matured late but grew magnificently into his role. He has a bone-crushing handshake, meticulously keeps score, and knows how the game is played. Mitt Romney's big mistake was believing his opponent for the Massachusetts Senate in 1994 was a batboy just because Rose Kennedy, when told of Teddy's childish antics, used to endlessly repeat, "Isn't he cute?" He may have started out a batboy, but Teddy's a catcher.

Patricia had a flair for Hollywood and glamour. She married Peter Lawford, a typical center fielder, and adopted and shared many of his traits, interests, and foibles. The Lawfords could make the big play, but they always had an aura of space about them. Together, Pat and Peter were the Kennedy clan center fielders.

Poor Rosemary was developmentally delayed, but being a Kennedy meant having to play in the game. She was their right fielder.

Eunice was never as multi-involved as the rest of the siblings and learned very early that she could not do as much as the rest so she focused on doing what she did well. She worked solely for improving the lot of the mentally disadvantaged; her crowning achievement is the Special Olympics. She's a third baseman.

The Smiths, Jean and her husband, Steve, played the keystone sack. They were the heart and core of the family and took care of the family business. Jack, Bobby, and Ted often ignored family duties and responsibilities to take care of politics, leaving day-to-day concerns to Jean and Steve. They were Boy Scouts; they handled second base.

Kathleen married an English Protestant and lived in England, alienated from her parents. She must have never played baseball.

Cheers was one of television's longest-running and most successful comedies, and the characters are as well known to most Americans as members of their own family. Each of the show's main characters personified the essential attributes of the nine positions on the baseball diamond. Here's who played what:

Character	Position	Attributes
Sam Malone	Pitcher	Conceited and charming
Frasier	First base	Frustrated and envious
Woody	Second base	Good, clean, and wholesome
Carla	Shortstop	Sassy, short, and crazy
Norm	Catcher	Rotund and opinionated
Coach	Third base	Dumb but dependable
Cliff	Right field	Inept, clumsy, dominant mother
Rebecca	Center field	Aloof, friendless
Diane	Left field	Spacey, liberal, smart

These are but two examples of the PIF Theory of Group Dynamics. The same principles apply to other television shows with large casts, such as *The Brady Bunch*, *L.A. Law*, *NYPD Blue*,

M*A*S*H, Taxi, and *Beverly Hills 90210,* as well as other professional groups, like the Supreme Court of the United States and the Joint Chiefs of Staff.

Selecting a group and then assigning the appropriate position to each member is an enjoyable pastime on long car rides, at cocktail parties, and in any situation when boredom threatens, such as after supper for inmates, after vespers for monks, or after court for sequestered jurors.

17

Practical Applications

The will to win is worthless if you don't get paid for it.

—*Reggie Jackson*

No theory has value without utility. In America, this means it ain't much good if it don't make money. That's why Newton never amounted to much. Gravity's a fine force no doubt, and the world is grateful to have it explained, but everybody with the possible exception of left fielders has about as much as they need; nobody wants to buy any more and if someone did, where would he or she put it? Anyway, it's only good for holding things together. Nitroglycerin, on the other hand, is useful for blowing things apart and that's why the Du Ponts, its inventors and merchants, are billionaires while Sir Isaac's heirs are street cleaners in Liverpool.

The Ryan Theory of Adolescent Development in American Males has countless practical uses and will eventually revolutionize our culture. For those who catch on quick, implementation of its implications will bring money and power.

In any circumstance, when many are to be called but one is to be chosen, the Ryan Theory is a shortcut to selecting the right candidate. Knowing a man's PIF and PIBO is like having a picture of his soul. While the questions themselves are innocuous, the answers reveal emotional strengths and weaknesses, physical attributes, personality traits, intellectual ranges, and levels of self-esteem.

Its fundamental limitation is that it applies only to males because youth baseball in our culture is primarily a gender-specific activity. Women have their own rites of initiation and it is left to some more knowledgeable social scientist to study the effects of field hockey, jump rope, and softball on the development of adolescent females.

In those cases where eight-year-old girls took their swings at the plate with the boys, the effects are similar and the application of the theory produces relatively accurate data. It is less exact because the peer and parental pressures on female players are less intense and the parental expectations are more realistic. Mom and Pop really don't believe their eight-year-old Monica is going all the way to The Show.

Just as no surgeon should operate without the aid of X rays, no male should be selected for any significant activity without revealing his PIF. At present, candidates for public office are allowed to list their former elected positions on the ballot. They should be required to list their former PIFs.

Public debates, door-to-door solicitations, and television political ads would be irrelevant and unnecessary if the ballot offered this choice:

Michael Dukakis, Second base   ————
Gary Hart, Pitcher   ————
Jerry Brown, Left field   ————

That's all voters would need to select the person most compatible with their own political philosophy and the person whose character they most admire.

Anybody who sells anything can make gobs of money by reading this book and applying its lessons in the workplace. Used car salesmen, for example. Customer walks onto the lot and starts to browse. Honest John hustles over and greets his prey. The typical sales pitch begins with small talk to learn something about the victim, the type of vehicle he wants, the size of his family, and the intended use of the vehicle. All that and more is produced with his answer to the question: "What position did you play?"

Suppose the quarry says he was a left fielder. The astute salesman brings him around back and points out a '71 tie-dyed Volkswagen van, sitting on blocks, ready for the junkyard. As quick as the shop can throw four wheels on the rusted hunk of tin, the left fielder is driving it out of the lot singing Joan Baez folk songs while Honest John counts his cash.

If the customer says he was a third baseman, our sophisticated metal pusher leads him to a pickup with chrome pipes and revs up the motor until the sound barrier crashes. If the third baseman hesitates for a minisecond, the salesman tells him to imagine how it will look with a gun rack in the back window. Six hours later, the third baseman drives away in the pickup. It took only ten seconds for the vision of the gun rack to cement the deal, but with the guy being a third baseman, it took half a day for him to fill out the paperwork.

Second basemen? Station wagons with easy-to-clean vinyl seats and roof racks for the bicycles, skis, and inner tubes. Just have to show him where to squeeze in the gear when he has fifteen screaming kids on their way to some family-and-friends adventure.

Shortstop? Motorcycle or sports car; anything that zooms.

Pitcher? Don't waste your time. He's slumming. Pitchers buy only the best. They don't take hand-me-down cars, clothes, or women.

First base? He'll be a hard sell and want an unbelievable deal. Double the asking price because he'll chop whatever you quote in half. Introduce him to the guys in the shop because he'll bring the car back for repairs twice a week until the warranty runs out.

Catcher? Anything with a gas-guzzling V8. Here's a chance to unload that Lincoln or Caddie—with all the extras—that gets three miles to a gallon.

Right field? The timid little mouse will buy anything if you back him into a corner, but if you want a happy customer, sell him something that was not made in Detroit: that's the home of the Tigers. Better to avoid the Japanese models, too. In fact, give the guy a break and make a friend for life by unloading a Volvo, Volks, or Saab or anything else from a country where baseball is unknown.

Center field? This is a difficult man of discriminating tastes. He must be down on his luck or he wouldn't be looking for used. Pretend you believe the car is for his teenage child or elderly father, his mistress, or the nuns who run the soup kitchen. Anybody but him.

Therapists should not be licensed until they have mastered the Ryan Theory. In fact, reeducation and recertification should be required for all practicing therapists. Freud's passé. What's id got to do with it? It's baseball, stupid. A man's experience in baseball preconditions him toward a particular neurosis. When life's circumstances become oppressive, the mental illness that will appear is 100 percent predictable if the known factor is the patient's baseball history. Once a therapist discovers a troubled soul's PIF, the diagnosis is obvious and can be discovered by reference to this chart:

Position Played	Affliction
Pitcher	Narcissism
First base	Paranoia
Second base	Overdependent personality
Shortstop	Impulsive personality disorder
Third base	Anal-compulsive personality
Catcher	Passive-aggressive disorder
Left field	Schizoid personality disorder
Center field	Satyriasis or claustrophobia
Right field	Agoraphobia
Nonplayer	Antisocial personality

In previous chapters, much was revealed about each player's foreseeable behaviors in love, romance, and marriage. For anyone who contemplates a long-term relationship with an American male, such reading should be mandatory. We'd have far fewer divorces if prospective wives were more aware of what to expect five, ten, or twenty years down the road. There should now be no surprises.

No social change would preserve family values better than modifying the words of traditional marriage vows from "Do you take this man as your lawful husband?" to "Do you take this first baseman as your lawful husband?" With this change, spouses would come, like cigarettes, with warning labels.

People who solicit contributions for charities would do well to prepare their appeals based on the targeted giver's PIF. They should identify who played what and then exchange data so each charity could zoom in on likely contributors. We suggest the following table would maximize the returns of all concerned.

Charity	Who Will Give
March of Dimes	Right fielders
Greenpeace	Left fielders
Boy Scouts of America	Second basemen

Heart Association	First basemen
Family Planning	Center fielders
National Rifle Association	Third basemen
Boys' Town	Catchers
Retired Actors Guild	Pitchers
Red Cross	Shortstops
Overseas Disaster Relief	Nonplayers

Incidentally, a pitcher will give to any organization which will call a press conference for the check presentation, and the contribution will be tripled for television coverage.

Not only charities but any business that relies on direct mail solicitations or catalog orders should prune and build its customer lists by focusing on PIFs. Victoria's Secret could increase its sales tenfold by identifying center fielders; L. L. Bean by zeroing in on left fielders; Brookstone on pitchers; Wal-Mart on third basemen; Sears on second basemen. For American capitalism, the good news is that PIF identifies who will buy what. Prosperity is just around the corner.

Employers, college admission committees, and headhunters could simplify their lives by eliminating applications, résumés, and letters of recommendation and simply asking for name, address, date of birth, social security number, and position played. The telephone company could provide an invaluable service to consumers by requiring PIFs in all ads accepted for their Yellow Pages.

So momentous are the long-term effects of PIF that the discoverers of the Theory are able to predict the short-term future for every player and nonplayer with a disclosed PIF. Horoscopes are now archaic. The stars are comparatively unreliable. A man's destiny is not determined by the influence of the planets but by the accomplishments of major leaguers who play his PIF. So strong is the subconscious attachment of a former player to his spiritual representative on his nearest team that his fortunes will rise and fall with that player's batting average and performance in the field. While the influence is more subtle in the off-season and most potent in pennant races, it is ever present. Soon all newspapers will be printing daily PIFascopes in lieu of horoscopes.

It does not require great vision to see that the revelation of the Ryan Theory of Adolescent Development in American Males will cause changes in the way decisions are made in the United States and wherever else in the world baseball is played. Finally, there is an explanation for behavior and an answer to the riddle of personality formation. A cultural revolution is certain to follow the publication of these findings. The Ryan Theory will reduce the American Revolution, the Industrial Revolution, and the Technological Revolution to mere blips on the radar screen of history.

The Theory's humble origins in T.J.'s Sports Bar by baseball-holics trying to come to grips with the baseball strike should not detract from its utility or importance to the psychological sciences. Many of the world's greatest discoveries occurred purely by accident. Columbus discovered the New World while looking for a shortcut to China. Newton discovered gravity by taking a nap in an apple orchard. Alexander Graham Bell discovered the secret of the telephone when he screwed up an experiment in his lab. Our neighbor discovered his wife was fooling around when he went home on his lunch hour to pick up a wrench. The impact of these discoveries on the course of human history was not diminished one bit by their inadvertence.

It does not matter a whit or a dollar how, when, where, or by whom a scientific breakthrough is achieved. If it stands up under scrutiny, if it passes the litmus test of truth, it must be accepted and acknowledged. Whether it's Bucky Dent or Mo Vaughn in the batter's box, if the ball is driven into the net above the Green Monster, it's a four-bagger.

Despite our innate humility and our lack of academic credentials or backgrounds in psychology, we feel our theory merits acclaim from scientists, admiration from the masses, and money from the government to continue our research, particularly the last since the baseball strike is over. We will graciously accept all awards, including the Nobel Prize in science; all grants, particularly a couple of those million-dollar Genius Prizes; and all medals from foreign powers, but all we truly hope to achieve from showing our ace in the hole is a vow from baseball owners and players that they will never again allow a lockout or a strike to cancel a single professional baseball game. That's because we're baseballholics and we gotta have it.

Appendix

Test for Determining PIF

Employers, women contemplating acceptance of proposals and/
or propositions, money lenders, college admissions personnel, re-
cruiters of spies, and people in need of doctors, lawyers, accoun-
tants, plumbers, electricians, carpenters, and other professional
personnel may wish to discreetly learn what position a man
played prior to making the critical decision. For such situated
people the following test is provided.

1. What did you ask the YBC before every game?
    A. How's my hair look?
    B. Who's pitching tonight?
    C. Will you buy us beer if we win?
    D. Can we use the Boudreau shift for lefties?
    E. Why can't I sit on a piano stool?

F. Can I have a ride home after the game?

G. Which one is third again?

H. Can I use your glove again?

I. I don't feel good. Can I go home?

2. What did the YBC ask you before every game?

A. Did Mom give you a good luck kiss?

B. You ready to go if Junior tires?

C. Are these your cigarettes?

D. What's the Boudreau shift?

E. Got your cup?

F. Who drove you here?

G. When's the last time your uniform saw soap?

H. Where's your own glove?

I. Why didn't you go before you came?

3. What did the YBC say to you as you took the field?

A. Give me the sunglasses.

B. Keep your toe on the bag.

C. Don't trip the base runners.

D. Keep the chatter going.

E. Give Junior a good target.

F. Take all the fair fly balls.

G. Do you know where to go?

H. Don't pick the dandelions.

I. Don't throw. Run it in.

4. What did the YBC say when you returned?

A. Good stuff, Junior.

B. Good glove, kid.

C. Good hustle, kid.

D. Good spirit, kid.

E. Good target, kid.

F. Good arm, kid.

G. Good duck, kid.

H. Have a good nap, kid?

I. Did you wet your pants again?

5. What did the YBC say as you went to bat?
   A. Bring 'em home, son.
   B. Set 'em up for Junior, Big Guy.
   C. Don't slide into first.
   D. Lay one down the third base line.
   E. No, you can't wear the mask.
   F. Just meet it. Don't try to kill it.
   G. Home plate is that way.
   H. Take the flowers out of your buttonholes.
   I. Whatever you do, don't swing.

6. Who convinced you to play organized youth baseball?
   A. My dad.
   B. My big brother.
   C. My probation officer.
   D. My grandpa.
   E. My pediatrician.
   F. My mom's boyfriend.
   G. My special ed teacher.
   H. My dad's boyfriend.
   I. My mom.

7. The night before a game you dreamed about:
   A. A no-hitter.
   B. Pitching.
   C. A brawl.
   D. An unassisted triple play.
   E. Same as always, chocolate fudge sundaes.
   F. Throwing out runners at first.
   G. Finding my base without help.

H. Same as always, Mozart's Second Violin Concerto.

I. Rain cancellations.

8. Who's your favorite player of all time?
   A. Jim Palmer.
   B. Dennis Eckersley.
   C. Shoeless Joe Jackson and Pete Rose.
   D. Jackie Robinson.
   E. Yogi Berra and Thurman Munson.
   F. Joe DiMaggio and Willie Mays.
   G. My brother, Big Sonny.
   H. Bill Lee.
   I. Gary.

9. What's your favorite memory of youth baseball?
   A. Breaking a kid's wrist with a fastball.
   B. Fanning the side in order in relief.
   C. Breaking a kid's leg with a slide.
   D. Playing it.
   E. Getting the ball to the pitcher in the air.
   F. The rides home from Coach.
   G. Finding my base without help.
   H. The sunsets in extra-inning games.
   I. The last game.

10. Complete this sentence: "If you can't beat 'em . . ."
    A. it ain't my fault.
    B. let me pitch.
    C. make 'em kill ya.
    D. give it your best shot.
    E. cheat.
    F. they ain't human.
    G. I don't know.

H. who cares?

I. let everybody go home.

Scoring the Test Results

Count the number of times each letter was chosen. One letter will be the answer more times than any other. Check the list below to find which position that letter represents. If one letter is not selected at least four times, the person taking the test has not been forthright with his answers. This means (1) he's lying because he never played baseball, (2) he's faking because he was a right fielder and does not want you to know it, or (3) he was a third baseman, can't read, and just guessed at the answers.

To determine which of these three situations applies to the suspect individual, give him the first two letters and ask him to spell *ox*. If he gets the answer wrong, he's a third baseman. If he spells it correctly, check the area where he took the test. If there is a puddle on the floor and the front of his pants is damp, he was a right fielder. If there is a lingering odor of flatulence in the air, he never played baseball.

A—Pitcher
B—First base
C—Shortstop
D—Second base
E—Catcher
F—Center field
G—Third base
H—Left field
I—Right field

Acknowledgments

We'd like to thank all those who supported us in the writing and research that went into this work, especially Judy, whose memories are woven throughout; Grammy, Molly, Maggie, and Bridie Ryan, who have long tolerated our baseballism; George Blake, Benny Wilson, Billy Larkin, Dean Whalen, and Ellis Landset, who laughed at earlier versions; Andy Ward and Kevin Sullivan, who haven't let their fondness for pinstripes interfere with friendship; John Smith and the patrons and staff of T.J.'s, who admitted where they played the game; ditto to Tom Rowan and the crew at Griffin's; Barbara Stenglein, who first told Luke he could write; Anna Kirwin, who encouraged Mike to keep writing; all the players and YBCs in Hatfield Youth Baseball 1978–1984; Jeff Dwyer for introducing our work to Gerry McCauley; Gerry for representing us; Bill Strachan and Henry Holt and Company for publishing us.

Acknowledgments

We'd also like to acknowledge our debt to Ken Burns, whose nine-part video *Baseball* not only motivated us to write this book but also is our source for much of the history and many of the celebrity quotes used in the text.

We finished work on this manuscript at 9:45 P.M. on September 20, 1995, the exact moment the Boston Red Sox clinched the Eastern Division Championship of the American League. We want to thank every man who played or worked for the Boston Red Sox from Ted Lepcio and John Kiley to Mo Vaughn and Rick Zawacki. You've given us joy, hope, and purpose and have been our common bond, the cement of our father-son relationship. Whatever tribulations and trials we've endured, we've always agreed on one critical issue: this is the year the Red Sox will finally win the World Series. We might not have been right yet, but we've always been loyal, and for second basemen being loyal is more important than being right.